Forgotten People

Collected memories of those who lived and worked in Basford Workhouse and Highbury Hospital, Nottingham, until the 1970s

Judy Bland

First published 2012
Bookworm of Retford
Spa Lane, Retford, Notts. DN22 6EA
01777 869224

www.bookwormretford.co.uk

A catalogue record for this book is available from the British Library.

ISBN 978 0955167 485

ACKNOWLEDGEMENTS

My thanks to Thelma Smith who, as a teenager in the 1970s, sat in the cold dark cellar of the hospital to produce the beautiful sketches.

Thanks also to Alan Gill B.A. for restoring the old photographs and for prompting me to seek publication of the work I began thirty-six years ago.

Finally, thank you to my husband Bob, our son, Alan and our daughter Elizabeth for helping turn the job I loved into a family affair.

CONTENTS

PREFACE

It is impossible to write of human tragedy and suffering without appearing to lay the blame at someone's door. However, in the following pages I have not sought to offend any individual, nor any groups of people, for the wasted lives which occurred as a result of their decisions or actions.

Human beings are simply pawns in a society, and will react according to the manner of the day in that period of time in which they live and work. Thus, if blame is to be laid anywhere, let it be upon society as a whole. In the latter half of the nineteenth century and the early years of the twentieth, society preferred to remain in ignorance of mental illness and subnormality, and was totally impervious to the poor. This had been the case for many centuries, and only recently has the sickness of the mind been widely explored, and the relief of poverty made available. Yet let us not judge our predecessors too harshly. Education was not so readily given or received; the rich lived in one world and the poor in another; and medicine did not progress in leaps and bounds as it does today. Instead, let us ensure that in years to come we are not guilty of the same crime - that of allowing, yes even encouraging, the degradation of our fellow men and women.

In 1976 when I first attempted to write an account of the suffering and heart-ache endured by the people spoken of herein, I used fictitious names to protect them. However, the people were alive and very real. I had no desire to turn them into public spectacles, and yet I believed that the public should be reminded of their existence, for when they passed away, so would part of our social history. As I write, it is now 2002 and these people no longer live, except in the hearts of those of us who cared for them. I believe that their story is still worth telling.

INTRODUCTION.

On returning to the nursing profession in 1974, following an eight year absence, I found myself caring for the mentally handicapped in a hospital dating back to 1815, originally a workhouse. Amongst my charges were men and women who had known the hospital as a Poor Law Institution. They had been certified as 'idiots', 'imbeciles', 'feeble-minded' persons, or 'moral defectives' in the early days of the century, and decades later, many years since workhouses became obsolete, they remained. The majority could not read, write, add simple figures, or spell simple words, but setting aside any lack of formal education, they had an abundance of experiences to share. Detained in an institution for persons of unsound mind until such a time that they felt that there was nowhere else to go, these forgotten people lived to serve what could only be described as a life sentence.

They remembered the 'basin haircut', the dreadful print frocks, lisle stockings, and the black, laced boots of the very early days; the long hours of scrubbing, laundering, and gardening in return for their keep. They recalled the loss of their children at an early age to other institutions, or, if they were very lucky, to adoptive parents; the segregation of the sexes to prevent further procreation; and the weekly supervised walks to town with 'paid hands', a name still used sometimes in 1974 to describe the nurses. They looked back on these walks, always in 'crocodile fashion', with the humble acceptance of those resigned to their fate.

Now, in 2002, I wonder how different their lives would have been had they been born into the society of today - a society where the pill and abortion are common words, and destitution is partially resolved by our social security system; where adult literacy and numeracy organisations abound, and government training schemes are open to all. We must hope that in years to come, history will not be repeated, and our hospitals for the mentally ill and mentally handicapped will not become simply refuges for the derelicts of another era. These people believed that the only escape from the sentence was to die, and back in the 1970s and 1980s when we lost one of our family - for so they were to those of us who cared - a dark cloud enveloped the ward until long after the funeral.

But changes were afoot. Some of these men and women did escape without having to die. They were moved into community homes and on to new beginnings. However, for many the transition was too difficult and came too late. Only the most resilient lived long enough to know life beyond the institution.

As you will read in the following pages, I have tried to reconstruct their lives from childhood to old age. In 1974

I could not have provided an ending, in 2002 I can. I dedicate these pages to those vulnerable people who asked for so little and gave, to me personally, so much.

JUDY BLAND.

THE BEGINNINGS OF THE POOR LAW AND THE ARRIVAL OF WORKHOUSES

Prior to the dissolution of the monasteries during the reign of Henry VIII, almshouses and church hospitals were responsible for the care of the sick, the aged, the destitute and their families. Not until the loss of this charity did the great numbers of unemployed vagrants and beggars come to the attention of the authorities. The State had to accept their presence in society, and left each Parish to care for its own derelicts. Due to the failure of this plan, some Local Authorities took the matter into their own hands and set a precedent for the State to follow.

London levied a compulsory poor rate, and offered poor relief through four Institutions — one for children, two for the sick, and the fourth, Bridewell, for able-bodied destitutes.

In 1572 a compulsory poor rate was accepted by the State, and in 1576 the Authorities were compelled to build more 'Bridewells', Houses of Correction, despite the fact that the ruling classes would not believe that anyone could be unemployed other than by his/her own fault. This action by the State constituted the basis of Poor Law administration until 1834. Henceforth the aged and the sick were to be cared for at home, helped by the levy, and the able-bodied were despatched to Houses of Correction to work.

The system worked successfully for most of the 17th century, and in 1631, by order of Charles I, a commission was set up to strengthen the administration. Alas, following the end of the personal government of Charles, greater freedom of action was returned to the Local Authorities. No longer was Poor Relief a national concern, it became parochial.

From this happening we inherit the phrase 'living on the parish' with its undertones of poverty, want and degradation. Voluntary Officials were appointed annually, their chief function being to maintain the poor as cheaply as possible and to de-populate the parish wherever they could to lessen the poor rate. Parochialism brought its problems, the main one being to determine to which parishes the people belonged. Unemployment led to necessary migration of labour, and those in search of work in the wealthier parishes were met with cold disapproval for fear that they should ever need relief. Originally a person belonged to the parish of his/her birth, or the one in which he/she had resided for a considerable length of time. This was a little vague due to the dislocations brought about by the Civil War.

To safeguard the wealthier parishes from an invasion of potential paupers, Parliament passed the Settlement Act 1662. This enabled authorised Justices of Peace to remove any new-comer, likely to need relief, from their parishes within forty days. This should not have been so, for with expanding trade and increasing town life, movement of labour should have been encouraged. Also by this Act, the overseers of a parish had far too much control over the masses of working people. 1697 saw the beginning of certification, whereby a person was given a certificate in his old parish and could remain elsewhere until he became chargeable. It was a hundred years before this became law passed by Parliament. If, however, a person was suspected of having small-pox, the scourge of this period, he/she was shuttled from parish to parish until the illness became intolerable. When that happened, the parish unfortunate enough to be housing him/her at that time was compelled to accept responsibility.

In the 18th century employment of the poor men, women, and children, was given under the supervision in houses specially built for the purpose -workhouses. A statute in 1723 authorised parishes to erect workhouses with residence as a condition of relief; thus becoming more economical by lowering the rates. At first there were separate buildings to house the different inmates - the sick, the aged, and the young -but by the end of the century, in every town, the groups were mixed under a common roof. The workhouse was a symbol of dread and despair, even to those who merely lived within its neighbourhood, because of the filth and disease it bred. Common decency was appalled at the treatment given to the inmates, and campaigners like William Wilberforce crusaded for better conditions. Others merely grumbled at the cost of poor relief.

In 1782 Parliament passed a law, drawn up by a humane, benevolent man called Gilbert, to restrict poorhouse accommodation to the old and sick, and to maintain the able-bodied in their own homes. The latter was accomplished by providing either work, cash supplements to inadequate wages, or full maintenance from rates. This was the beginning of outdoor relief. Years later the rates for the poor were arranged at the Pelican Inn in Speenhamland, and were called the Speenhamland System. These rates were legalised by Parliament in 1796 and remained operative until 1834. The system came in for a lot of criticism - a rapidly increasing population, some said, because of the bounties given. None considered that this may have been due to falling death rates as a result of better conditions. In any case the wealth of the country was expanding rapidly enough to cope with the cost of relief.

In 1834 the Poor Law Amendment Act was passed following a report by a Royal Commission. This Act withdrew outdoor relief and only gave relief to the inmates of the workhouses. Parishes were grouped into Unions, and elected Boards of Guardians replaced the Overseers. Over all was a Poor Law Commission, three members with extensive powers of control. It is interesting here to note that one gentleman, namely George Nicholls, of this Commission, the first of its kind, was from a small Parish in Nottinghamshire, my home town, where he had been ruthless at his job in his efforts to benefit the rate-payers. Could this workhouse be the one you are to read about - it may be so. With outdoor relief abolished it was obvious that the occupants of workhouses would increase, and the suffering and want was beyond the imagination. Dickens abhorred the system; Hovell called it a 'mass demonstration of misery', and Carlyle said that the Law suggested that whosoever will not work ought not to live. However, ruthless as the system was, by the end of 1847 financial economies and the reduction of paupers had been achieved, at a cost of 'crushed misery in the depths'.

All workhouses had mixed inmates until 1861, when it was indignantly declared that there should be separate houses for the children, the old, and the infirm. In trying to apply this theory there was total failure. Towards the end of the 19th century and the beginning of the 20th, treatment of the old and sick was relieved at public expense, with Trade Unions and Friendly Societies actively supporting the forgotten cause.

Poor Law Dispensaries appeared in London in the 1880s, and throughout the provinces at a slightly later date, becoming almost countrywide by 1900. The children were to benefit enormously, although they had been left in the care of ageing inmates never breathing fresh air until as late as 1906. The tiny babes had been sharing accommodation with female tramps, and yet it was not until 1915 that the youngsters were compulsorily removed from workhouses. Once the seeds of benevolent progress had been sown, Assurance Companies helped to speed up the process. Weekly collections ensured financial help at a minimal cost. However, there was still a need for State participation in Social Insurance, a scheme already operating efficiently in Germany. It was not until 1908 that non-contributory Old Age pensions were made payable, and 1912 before the first part of the

National Insurance Act was in operation. Labour Exchanges were widespread by 1909, with 'dole' money becoming available in 1921. Originally the benefit of an unemployment claim was limited to 15 weeks in any one year. 1925 saw the beginning of a contributory pension scheme to cover widows, orphans, and old age pensioners.

In 1931, when unemployment reached its zenith, the Public Assistance Committee was born. The expansion of National Insurance reduced the numbers of those claiming relief under the Poor Law, but there were so many agencies concerned with administration. In 1941 a committee led by Sir William Beveridge surveyed the whole system, and their report led to the seedlings from which our Social Security Department of today grew. A chief addition at this time led to legislation of Children's Allowances, and it is an interesting fact that a National Health Service was suggested in 1942, and was rejected due to opposition from the medical profession. As we know, this came into being a few years later and has been a great asset to all of us.

Fig.1 The Workhouse of the Basford Incorporation; established in 1815. It became the workhouse of the Basford Union in 1836.

FROM WORKHOUSE TO HOSPITAL

Theirs is yon house that holds the Parish-poor,
Whose walls of mud scarce bear the broken door,
There where the putrid vapours, flagging, play,
And the dull wheel hums doleful through the day,
There children dwell who know no mother's care,
Parents, who know no children's love, dwell there.
Heart-broken Matrons on their joyless bed,
Forsaken wives, and mothers never wed,
Dejected widows with unheeded tears,
And crippled age with more than childhood fears,
The lame, the blind, and, far the happiest they,
The moping idiot, and the mad-man gay.
Here too the sick their final doom receive,
Here brought, amid the scenes of grief, to grieve,
Where the loud groans from some sad chamber flow,
Mixed with the clamours of the crowd below,
Here sorrowing, they each kindred sorrow scan,
And the cold charities of man to man,
Whose laws indeed for ruin'd age provide,
And strong compulsion plucks the scrap from pride,
But still that scrap is brought with many a sigh,
And pride embitters what it can't deny.

George Crabbe (18th century)

Having read these lines from 'The Village' by 19th century poet, George Crabbe, it would seem unnecessary to elaborate on the conditions to be found in workhouses. Yet, more detail must be given if we are to appreciate fully the lives of the inmates, the pitiful state shared by so many.

The workhouses were called 'Bastilles'. The inmates were treated with abominable cruelty, suffering all manner of human degredation and the total loss of their self-respect. The Overseers were immune to the humiliation they meted out, and harshly indifferent to the feelings of those who had fallen upon bad times. Although the Commission had recommended separate workhouses for each class of the poor, this was not so. They were all thrown together into the same garbage bin. Under one roof could be found decaying bodies and unwanted humanity, be they child or adult, sane or lunatic. Money was withheld to keep the 'Bastilles' as uncomfortable as possible.

Brutal rules governed residence. It was 1842 before married couples were allowed to be together - in fact whole families were kept apart. The same hours, the same meals, and the same work applied to all the inmates, except children under 7 years old, and the very old. Meals were taken in silence; smoking was forbidden; and there were no books, not even Bibles. Those people who had toiled long and hard for many years, only to be thrown out of work by a slump, were compelled to keep company with criminals, prostitutes, and lunatics. Exercise was non-existent, since there were no fast rules to govern this. Visitors were only allowed at the discretion, and in the presence of, the Master or Matron. Until 1842 parents were not even able to see their own children, who were quite possibly in the same workhouse.

Air-space and lighting were unheard of until 1868. It was in that year too that old, as in aged, inmates were first given 'benches with backs, of sufficient width to offer reasonable comfort', and the children were allowed small arm-chairs. How they must have suffered during the years before! No-one was allowed to leave the workhouse except on business - this included the able-bodied and the 'loose women' to leave at will, returning only when they needed support. This rule of virtual imprisonment was relaxed to permit Church attendance, or, in the case of the very young, to attend school. Those to benefit the least when conditions began to improve were the people labelled as 'Mental Defectives'.

In 1848 the Commissioners of Lunacy, men trained in law and medicine, began a series of investigations into workhouses. They accepted that the Mental Defectives had a malady requiring special treatment, and advised the Board of Guardians to despatch many of them to asylums. Only, 'the idiot, imbecile paupers who were tractable and harmless' remained. Medical knowledge was increasing in every other field, but there had been little advance in the methods of dealing with the Mentally Defective who were not dangerous enough to be removed to asylums. Thus they were left to rot in the workhouses, and it was estimated that in the workhouse, now hospital, of which I write, 10% of the residents between 1846 and 1872 were mental defectives.

By 1840 there were over 600 workhouses in England, harbouring what some saw as human refuse, and spreading fear of disease through over-crowding and lack of sanitation.

Highbury in Bulwell, Nottinghamshire was the name of the hospital where I worked on my return to nursing in 1974. It was built as a workhouse in 1815, during the reign of George III. For 187 years, spanning nine monarchies, it has been, and is still being used for the service of the public. Here no doubt would have been offered, in the early years, the same cruel fate as at all the other 'Bastilles' throughout the country. The addition of the Poor Law Dispensary came in 1901, with paid nurses at a ratio of 1: 65 inmates, and the same stringent rules of residence would apply. When the old Poor Law finally died in the late 1920s this workhouse became the County Certified Institution. Cutlery can still be found bearing that dreadful label, a constant reminder of a not-too-distant past.

THE WORKHOUSE CELLARS

In 1974 these cellars were as dark and eerie as they were nearly two centuries ago, indeed they are still the same today in 2002. An earthy smell pervaded the atmosphere, and the damp chilled the flesh. Spiders scurried around in the half- light, and cob-webs clung to the body. Even though the cellars were then lit by recently added light bulbs, it was easy to be transported, by imagination, back in time, nearly two hundred years, to when the workhouse was new and awaiting the arrival of streams of pathetic souls whose misfortune it was to cross the threshold into the world of despair and degradation; to stand and realise that in the bright, clean wards above, there were men and women who knew this world and were there to tell the tale.

The next decade in the life of Highbury is shrouded in mystery, but in 1938, a local G.P. and a Consultant Psychiatrist separated the young Mentally Handicapped from the older residents, and despatched them to other hospitals throughout the country. Here it was expected that they would have better opportunities for the future. In 1948 the N.H.S. took over the responsibility of care, and the Institution became Highbury Hospital. Many of the residents I came to know so well were admitted that same year, from other Institutions in England. Others had lived there long before the Poor Law ended, during the latter years of the workhouse. Their lives had been ones of hard work and dejection, and this did not change overnight simply because the Institution had become a hospital. The long hours of laundering, gardening, and cleaning - not as we know it today - were to continue for many years to come.

Payment, if any, was a pittance - often in the form of sweets. Clothes were issued, and sewn and patched beyond belief before they could be condemned and replaced. Outings were 'en-bloc' and heavily supervised; males and females were not allowed to mix socially - in fact, life was as austere during the first years of the NHS. as it was before.

Naturally local and public awareness was aroused, and it was suggested that many of the residents who were detained could be elsewhere, and that they were being used as cheap labour. The long hours of toil had to end, although in many cases this meant that the residents were left to vegetate, for they only knew how to work. Very gradually over the years to follow this forced inactivity was replaced by educational classes, social activities, recreational pursuits, and entertainment. Alas for some of the older residents, these changes had come too late, and they were unable to cope. Release into the community was not considered too enthusiastically because so many of the older folk had been institutionalised for decades, and there was nowhere else for them to go. The pittance eventually gave way to the Non-contributory Invalidity Pension, providing a bank account and pocket money, and the hospital clothing issue was phased out and replaced by private clothing, chosen in most cases by the old folk themselves. The aged buildings of the hospital were being upgraded in

1974, and although it took a long time, the changes were immense. Today, in 2002, there are purpose-built housesfor the residents with learning difficulties, protection of their human rights, and the freedom, where possible, for them to make their own choices. What a long way we have come from the workhouse!

The ward, the home of most of the residents you are to read about, was part of the original Workhouse, and in the days of the early N.H.S. was known as the 'M.D. Block', housing those labelled Mental Defectives. Living here were 26 ladies, many of whom had known no other home for 40 years or more and had simply exchanged some other Institution for this one. As in most old buildings used for hospitals, there were two storeys, separated by one wide, straight stair-case - very steep - and another, narrow, curved, and even steeper. The upstairs consisted of two dormitories divided by a passage along which there were three individual bedrooms, one double and two single. These rooms were used by the more able in 1974, but in days gone by were used to 'confine and punish' the naughty!

The lower storey was made up of a day-sitting room, an office for the nursing staff, a clinic, and sleeping accommodation for the more severely disabled and handicapped, a bathroom and a large dining/kitchen area. Toilet facilities were situated throughout. Comfortable furniture and modern amenities were in abundance in the 1970s, and the effort to make the ladies comfortable and the ward as home-like as possible was evident to all.

Within the hospital itself there was a little evidence to remind us of the workhouse days: innumerable mazes of cellars lay beneath the wards, with huge sinks, used for salting pork, and ramps down which the barrels were rolled in the days of the Master. Large foundation stones distinguished the additional buildings erected in 1901, showing the names of the members of the Board of Guardians, the Medical Officer, the Architect, and the Master himself. A huge circular stone marks the original entrance to the workhouse, marked, ERECTED MDCCCXV.

At the top of the long, long drive which led to the entrance of the original buildings of the workhouse stood what looked like a small cottage. This was the Lodge, and once past here the streams of pathetic humanity whose misfortune it was to become inmates, would have known the sense of impending doom. In my days at Highbury the Lodge was used as the telephone exchange for the hospital, until it was demolished to make way for a car park and ambulance drop-off point to serve the purpose-built Day Centre for those with learning difficulties.

Half-way down the drive was another larger building. Originally this was the 'doss house', where in those early years the able-bodied who had employment could pay a pittance to have a bed for the night and still carry on with their work during the day. In the 1970s this building was used for ante- natal appointments, and when the Maternity Services were moved off site, it became a storage area for old medical records, and at one point housed the Pharmacy. Just past the old doss house was the boiler house, although I am not sure whether this was the original one. The stone and brickwork certainly matched that of the workhouse and not the buildings added at a later date. On down the drive-way from here stood Laurel Ward, but there was still quite a walk to reach the main entrance of the workhouse. Laurel ward stood at a right angle to the huge door which would have closed heavily behind the inmates.

A different ward, set slightly apart and housing the elderly with physical illnesses, was originally used for the meeting place of the Board of Guardians, and it was here where decisions were made as to whether or not to grant an appeal for release, or extend a given release on license at the request of the Social Worker in charge of a particular inmate.

Buildings and architecture are very interesting, but this is a book about forgotten people, so before I introduce you to the ladies individually, let me explain how many of them came to be there at all.

Of the twenty six ladies living on Laurel ward, nineteen were certified as Mental Defectives until 1958. In maybe half a dozen cases, setting aside the dreadful label, I am sure it was a necessary evil, but for the remainder living there it was a long, hard sentence to serve for staggering, unbelievable reasons, especially thinking in terms of the society of today. In the first instance, applications for their detention, either under guardianship or in an Institution, came from various sources - parents, recommended guardians, social workers, or the Local

Education Authority. Reasons for detention includedbeing neglected or being guilty of neglect, being uneducable, poverty, destitution, pregnancy out of wedlock, or simply being a nuisance at home. If this were allowed to happen today, two thirds of our population would be shut away, and a great number of professional people would be out of work!

Following the application, an assessment was made of the victim's intellect by a doctor not necessarily connected with any form of mental handicap. The methods used to assess left a lot to be desired compared to the advanced techniques used today to determine a person's I.Q. Simple spellings were asked: cat, dog, horse, and certificate (a quick survey in 1974 showed that 35% of the nursing staff could not spell the latter!). Simple arithmetic was also used, including the management of money e.g. how many half-crowns make a pound? Since a good proportion of the victims were destitute, it is unlikely that they saw enough half-crowns to make a pound. Considering the failure in the early days, it was remarkable how easily the ladies adapted to decimalisation. A common question of general knowledge to be asked was: how far is it to New York? One of the ladies from Laurel Ward suggested that it was twice as far as to London, a logical answer since travel was in the realms of fantasy for the poor in the early days of the 20th century. She was diagnosed as feeble-minded in 1920 and had been in the hospital ever since. How tragic that a life-time could be wasted for such simplicity. Following the assessment, an appeal was made to a Justice of the Peace for the Lunacy Act 1890 for an order of detention. Upon the granting of the order the life sentence began.

Fig.2 This sketch shows the entrance to the cellar which was the larder of the Workhouse. The stairway was curved, narrow and very steep. The centre of each step was well- trodden, in some cases almost worn away. To the left of the arch were two small rooms which, being completely of stone and situated below ground level, acted as refrigerators in early days.

Fig.3 This sketch shows the ramp, down which the victuals were rolled in the early days of the Master. Like all workhouses, Highbury was virtually self-sufficient, having ample ground in which to grow all manner of vegetables, and certainly enough inmates to toil on the land.

Fig.4 This is the corridor of the main cellar. Note the thickness of the walls and the huge heavy door.

Fig.5 This table was the butchers slab. In the background can be distinguished the stone slabs found on each wall of the cellar, and the arc of the wall and ceiling show the shape and height of this rounded vault.

Fig.6 This sketch shows the old limestone bath, though it cannot be decided for what purpose it was used. Encased by brickwork, it is hoped that it was not used for bathing.

Fig.7 The keeping of pigs was most common to most workhouses. The fattening of their own animals for slaughter lessened the cost of feeding the inmates. This sink was the one in which the pork was salted.

CITY OF ______________________.

MENTAL DEFICIENCY ACT 1913.

ORDER MADE UNDER SECTION 7 (1) OF THE ABOVE ACT VARYING A PREVIOUS ORDER AND SENDING DEFECTIVE TO AN INSTITUTION.

WHEREAS ON THE__________DAY OF_________19_________

AN ORDER WAS MADE BY__________, A JUSTICE OF

THE PEACE FOR THE CITY OF_________APPOINTING_________

______________OF_______________

IN THE CITY OF_______________TO BE THE GUARDIAN OF

_________________, A DEFECTIVE WITHIN THE

MEANING OF THE MENTAL DEFICIENCY ACT, 1913, BEING (1)_____

_______AND WHEREAS THE SAID___________

HAS BECOME UNSUITABLE FOR GUARDIANSHIP.

AND WHEREAS THE COUNCIL OF THE CITY OF____________

AND THE RELATIVES OR OTHER PERSON WHO PRESENTED THE

ORIGINAL PETITION AND THE PARENT OR GUARDIAN OF THE

SAID______________ HAVE BEEN GIVEN THE OPPORTUNITY

OF BEING HEARD.

NOW THEREFORE, I _________UPON APPLICATION MADE

TO ME BY__________OF__________

AN OFFICER OF THE LOCAL AUTHORITY OF THE CITY OF________

__________, DO HEREBY ORDER THAT THE SAID_______

WHO IS (2)________________________________

BE REMOVED TO________________________________

DATED THIS________DAY OF_________19________.

SIGNED____________________________

A JUSTICE OF THE PEACE FOR THE CITY OF

_________SPECIALLY APPOINTED

UNDER THE LUNACY ACT, 1890.

(FORM D/3) F.

(INSTITUTION)

OR

NAME OF (CERTIFIED HOUSE)

OR

(DWELLING OF GAURDIAN)

ORDER BT BOARD OF CONTROL CONTINUING ORDER OR AUTHORITY FOR DETENTION.

____

____

NAME OF PATIENT____

DATE OF ORDER ON WHICH DETAINED__________________________________

AURTHORITY FOR DETENTION____

DATE AT WHICH ORDER WILL EXPIRE IF NOT CONTINUED__________________

THE BOARD OF CONTROL, HAVING CONSIDERED THE REPORTS AND CERTIFICATES WITH REGARD TO THE ABOVE NAMED PATIENT, PARTICULARS OF WHICH ARE SET OUT BELOW, AND THE MEANS OF CARE AND SUPERVISION WHICH WOULD BE AVAILABLE FOR HER/HIM IF SHE/HE WERE DISCHARGED, AND BEING SATISFIED THAT THE CONTINUENCE OF THE ABOVE NAMED AURTHORITY FOR DETENTION IS REQUIRED IN HER/HIS INTERESTS TO HEREBY ORDER SAME TO BE CONTINUED

FOR_____________FROM THE_______________DAY OF _________________.

SEALED WITH OUR COMMON SEAL THIS__________DAY OF___________.

WITNESS:-________________________________

SECRETARY TO THE BOARD OF CONTROL.

____

REPORTS AND CERTIFICATES REFERRED TO IN THE ABOVE ORDER.

SPECIAL REPORT DATED______________________________

VISITORS OF INSTITUTIONS FOR DEFECTIVES FOR THE COUNTY_______________

____

SPECIAL REPORT AND CERTIFICATE DATED_____________________________

MEDICAL PRACTITIONER (MEDICAL OFFICER FOR THE ABOVE NAMED INSTITUTION)

This is a photograph of Mary, my dear friend, who died in my arms in 1980 as a result of pulmonary embolism. It was taken in 1949 shortly after Mary's transferral to

Highbury, from the Institution in Derbyshire. She believed that the photo was taken on a Sunday, for despite the inevitable print overall, she is not wearing the black laced-up boots she wore for working. Mary is smiling in the picture … Mary smiled a lot, even in the face of great hardship, and she never lost her sense of humour through all the years that I knew her.

MARY AND EVELYN.

In 1976 when I first thought of writing about the forgotten people, Mary was a frail old lady using a walking - frame to help her move about the ward. Her tall, once erect body was bent in an effort to get her legs moving; her face had a pinched look, and her sad, glazed eyes belied the possession of an alert mind, a sharp wit, and a dry sense of humour. How she had changed physically in the past few months since she had fallen during the night and fractured her hip!

Prior to the fracture, Mary was always the first person to greet me every morning on Laurel Ward. She had made herself responsible for the protection of my nurse's cap, and was sure of being awake when I came on duty at 7.30.a m. She was a well-made lady with short grey hair, uncurled because she preferred it that way, and a lively smile to start every day.

This photograph shows Mary and Evelyn preparing for the Easter bonnet parade. Every Easter Monday a Bonnet Parade was held in the concert hall of the hospital, followed by a dance. Mary would never wear a bonnet - she wasn't into that sort of things, but she always went along to support her friend. The concert hall was the focal point for social life for many years - dances were held regularly, afternoon sessions of Bingo were arranged, and films were shown once a week on a large screen which was placed on the stage.

This picture is a particular favourite of mine. A local young man was trying to make a living out of photography, and he came to the hospital to ask if he could 'practise on us'. It was a lovely day and we went out on to the field adjacent to Laurel Ward, and Mary and I stood to have this picture taken. I think that it captures beautifully the mutual affection we had for each other.

The injury had robbed Mary of her former vitality, but her memory remained unimpaired. She could still remember her early days 'inside', making tea in the 'big copper urn' for the other inmates; scrubbing the dayroom floor before breakfast because ' in them days we din't hey rugs', and rushing to get to work in the laundry or to scrub the floors in the 'Infirmary', later to become maternity wards. Mary had always known how to work!

In her youth Mary had a job as a paper sorter until things went wrong. Mary came to Highbury in 1949, diagnosed as feeble-minded. In 1922 she had given birth to an illegitimate girl. The pregnancy put an end to her paid employment. She was despatched by order to an Institution in Blackburn, and then removed to a second one in Nottinghamshire later in the same year. The move to her third Institution, in Derbyshire, came four years after her original admission, namely in 1926.This was the way of life for the poor and unfortunate of the early 1920s and before - to be shuttled from corner to corner like unwanted rubbish until some refuse collector put it tidily away.

Unknown to Mary, her daughter had been placed in the same Institution in Derbyshire as a small baby and was still there at the time of Mary's transferral to Highbury in 1949. It was many years later that mother and daughter were to meet for the very first time. Since that re-union in the late 1950s gave so much pleasure to both women, it would be wrong at this point if praise was not given to the diligent social worker who brought it about.

In conversation Mary would jokingly tell of her daughter's conception (in a hay-stack) although she would not or could not recall the name of the father. She would simply say that he was well-off. She would refer to the 'owd bonnets and shawls' used for church in the different institutions, and the 'owd patched frocks' and black boots worn for working. These boots were changed for working in the laundry, where clogs were worn because of the depth of the water in which the inmates had to stand. Mary liked scrubbing the infirmary best of all, because the water in the laundry made her feet 'rheumaticky'. She talked enthusiastically about 'sticking' (the term used for collecting fire-wood to keep the fires going in the laundry) because the inmates went out alone to 'stick'. Mary had been in many a queue for sweets as payment for her hard labour, and would gasp with wonder at the money she received at this time. For year upon year she had worn old, patched clothes, supplied by the Institution, and initially by the N.H.S. and it was very difficult to persuade her that new garments were for wearing, and not for storing away for high days and holidays.

Although virtually a prisoner to her arm-chair, Mary was a sensible old lady who wrote regularly to her daughter, and occasionally visited her in the Institution in Derbyshire — by this time a Hospital for the Mentally Subnormal, a new word being used to replace the previously used Defective. Mary took an interest in a younger resident of Laurel Ward, a difficult girl with Down's syndrome, although she could no longer actively participate in her care. Mary could be your grandmother, or mine, and yet here she was, 58 years in an institution as a result of an illegitimate child.

Mary's life had been a tragic one; she paid dearly for her moment of folly. The life of her daughter Marjorie was equally tragic, for she too spent the same 58 years hidden away from Society paying for the circumstances of her birth. She, however, was still comparatively young and able to benefit from the educational and social opportunities offered in the late 1970s and onwards. Marjorie could read and write, and was 'employed' on the ward where she resided. She was quite a bright woman, always presentable but the years of Institution life had taken its toll and it was highly unlikely that she would ever live without supervision.

As for Mary herself, she died in 1980 following a second operation on her hip. She died in my arms from a pulmonary embolism. I lost a very good friend, as did Evelyn who had shared a double bedroom with Mary for a very long time.

Evelyn was born in 1911, and was readmitted to the Highbury in 1947 - readmitted because she had already lived there as a child; diagnosis was feebleminded! She was removed from her parents' care at the age of eight due to being neglected. They too were described as feeble-minded, and parental care was given to the Board of Guardians of Highbury when it was the County Institution. There was still a row of cottages at the hospital in 1974 which were originally used for children such as Evelyn, although by then they had become changing rooms for the nursing staff and accommodation for the doctors. My own mother could remember the 'workhouse' or 'union kids' as they were called when she was a child; she used to see them trotting in a crocodile line to the local Church, all dressed alike and looking very much the pathetic little beings they were. Unless these children were adopted, it was here they lived until they became adults. Then it was transferral to a 'grown-up' Institution. Such was the fate of Evelyn. She attended school in the city of Nottingham, but at the age of 16 was certified as Mental Defective, the cause stated as probably being due to a fall from a bus on her way to the school. In 1927 Evelyn was transferred to an Approved Home in Uxbridge, having become an adult and still unwanted. Here she stayed until 1934, as the Matron's maid. She undertook many domestic tasks, but it was stated that she could not work without supervision. At this time, Evelyn's mother died and her father was also placed in an Institution, though not the same one as his daughter.

In 1935 Evelyn was moved again - this time to another Approved Home in Painswick. Again she became the maid of the Matron, and was quite happy in her work, but there was still a further move to come....to Highbury in 1947. Evelyn had come a complete circle.

Although Evelyn could not read and write (except her name) she was by far the most intelligent resident on Laurel Ward. She cleaned the bedroom she shared with Mary until it gleamed; she dressed well, and spent her money wisely.

Until they left the area, Evelyn used to visit a local family and perform light domestic duties for them in return for friendship and the occasional small gift. When they moved house Evelyn was distraught, and once again alone. However, the family kept in touch with her, and she spent quite a few holidays with them. In 1977 she even braved the task of making the journey alone, over 150 miles.... no mean feat for a woman who had been diagnosed as feeble-minded and shut away from the outside world for sixty years. To try and compensate for the loss of what Evelyn called her ' job' with the family, she was asked to help the domestics who cleaned the Nurses' Home, but she confessed that it wasn't the same.

Evelyn was of small stature, scrupulously clean and well-mannered - not very popular with her peers because she kept herself to herself and they saw this as snobbery. She enjoyed the privacy of the bed-room she shared with Mary, and each morning at 7.30a.m. she could be found shaking mats, dusting ornaments, and washing the floor until it shone - always afraid, despite reassurances to the contrary, that she would lose the privilege.

How sad for Evelyn, and what a waste of a life-time! Neglected by her parents, considered incapable of being educated, the loss of her mother, and her friends to another area - a succession of events leading to detention and adding to its severity. How lacking in fore-sight must our fore-runners have been not to have recognised the potential hidden within Evelyn! Wandering around the local streets and shops she could have been anyone's next door neighbour, and the tragedy is that Evelyn was intelligent enough to know this.

It seemed that Evelyn was destined to live out her life in Highbury, but the words “Community Care” were on everyone’s lips, and Evelyn was considered an ideal candidate for a trial. She was transferred to a very large, overpopulated local Residential Home in 1983.

The early days of Community Care left a lot to be desired for those who had been ‘institutionalised’ for so many years and were only just becoming accustomed to the efforts made to improve their daily living. In the Residential Home, Evelyn’s freedom was curtailed: no more trips to the shops by herself; she missed the intimacy with the nursing staff who had been her family for so long; she lost her individuality which had taken so many years to find. In short, Evelyn became more of a number than a person when she entered the door of the Home. The hard work and patience from the nurses on Laurel Ward who had gradually built up Evelyn’s confidence over a long period of time was brushed away in an instant.

Sadly Evelyn died within three weeks of leaving Highbury. The death certificate stated that she’d had a stroke. I have to ask myself if there are medical words for crushed spirit and broken heart?

Thanks once again to our local photographer, here is a picture of myself with Maria. She was 70 years old when the photo was taken, and one would never guess by looking at her that she had spent many long years in Institutions - years of very hard work. Notice the length of her skirt! How times had changed since she had worn the inevitable print frocks, almost ankle length. My own short frock, very unprofessional, is due to the fact that it was a hand-me-down from a retired Ward Sister who was a foot shorter than me!

MARIA AND HENRY

Not until the early 1970s, due to enlightened ideas in the treatment of Mental Handicap, were the male and female residents allowed to associate freely. They mixed socially at the hospital dances, film shows, and any other social activity arranged. Barriers were broken down, and as was natural, romances flourished. Relationships were easy and companionable in spite of the years of being kept apart.

In 1977 Maria was 69 years old, and two years previously had become 'engaged' to Henry, some years her junior. He had bought her a solitaire engagement ring and we gave a party on the ward to celebrate the occasion. Pomagne stood in ice in a dressings bucket, flowers stood on the tables, food was abundant, and both Maria and Henry were given a present. Needless to say, they were dissuaded from rushing into marriage because of the management problems in the old buildings of the workhouse. As both of them had been cared for in Institutions for a very long time, it seemed hardly likely that they could cope with any other life, even together and in love. Nevertheless, the solitaire ring was a great source of pride to Maria, and proved that we were heading in the right direction with our new concept of care - namely to make life 'inside' as near normal as possible. Maria was born in 1908, one of five children. Of the five she alone remained alive. One died in infancy, one died at 16 as a result of burns, one died on active duty in the 1914-18 war, and the fourth died in child-birth. Maria's father committed suicide at the age of 53, and her mother died in 1973 in a Mental Hospital in Derbyshire, where she had been a patient for a number of years. Mother had played an important role in Maria's life, giving up only as a result of her own advancing years and ill-health.

Very little is known of Maria's early life prior to her admission to Highbury in 1934 from a Public Assistance Institution, where it was alleged that she was feeble-minded. Mother gave a few facts but these may not be completely accurate, although Maria tells almost the same story. She attended school until the age of fourteen, was able to read and write, and held a job for seven years after leaving school. She lost her job as a result of an industrial dispute, and was forced to claim poor relief.

Maria gave birth to an illegitimate child in 1923 at the age of fifteen, and the two of them, she and her child, remained at home with Maria's parents so that she could continue to work. It was in 1933 that Maria lost her job, the home was no more, and the parents were placed in the Public Assistance Institution in Shardlow. Maria was herself certified and sent to a local Institution for Mental Defectives. It is not recorded on paper but we could safely assume that her daughter, for all we knew of the child was that it was a female, was also placed in care, whereabouts unknown.

On admission to her first Institution Maria was described as head-strong, in need of care and training, but the main factor for her detention was that she was without visible means of support. There is no record of her parent's release, but this must have been so, for in 1945, exactly eleven years after Maria's transferral to Highbury, she was released on licence to the care of her mother, father having killed himself by this time. The Social Worker's reports were favourable on each home visit, and licence continued to be extended until 1953.

Maria and her mother shared a three bed-roomed cottage in Breaston, Derbyshire - sparsely furnished but very clean. Mother did domestic work at a nearby Training College and earned £1 per week; her widow's pension was 26 shillings (£1.25) and this was supplemented by Maria's wage of 30 shillings per week (£1.50) for domestic duties to families in the area. Rent was 5 shillings and five pence, approximately 28p today. Maria's employers respected her and she worked well.

Her chief family, for she had as many as four to 'do' for, left Derbyshire and Maria's wage dropped dramatically. At one point the social worker suggested that Maria was being exploited, earning only 13 shillings (£1.15) for 10 hours hard cleaning. Exploitation was very common in those days since the alternative to paid employment was pauperism and re-entry into the institution where the chances of exploitation were greatly increased, or so a good many people believed. In Maria's case the social worker appealed for an increase in pay, but this was refused, which meant that Maria and her mother were living virtually on the bread-line. They spent their leisure time visiting relatives, attending chapel, or at the cinema on very rare occasions. Maria was never allowed out alone, except to go to work- again to prevent procreation, although towards the end of her licence her child-bearing years were almost over.

In 1951 the social worker suggested a release from the detention order and mother was willing to accept Maria on a permanent basis. What would have happened to Maria if the request had been granted? We shall never know, for the Medical Officer in charge of Maria refused by reason of 'uncertainty regarding the future of the patient'. Licence continued, but Maria rebelled against the strict discipline — not unnatural in a woman of 43 years old. She began to go out alone, only to the cinema or to visit relatives, but mother felt compelled to report this to the social worker, and in 1953 he recommended 'early removal to Highbury'.

In 1958 Maria was de-certified and her mother was approached regarding her discharge. By this time mother was old and in poor health, so she had to refuse, and Maria stayed in care because there was nowhere else for her to go. At the time I began to think of telling Maria's story, she was carrying out light domestic duties on the ward, and enjoying the freedom she shared with Henry. They went out shopping most days, or simply walking, arm in arm like any other elderly couple. Maria would never tolerate make-up, but had her hair set regularly and looked neat and tidy all of the time.

Circumstances were cruel to Maria, as to many of our families, but at least she found romance in her declining years. She overcame her thirteen-hour shifts in the institution laundry; she forgot that her knees were like emery boards as a result of long, long hours of scrubbing; and as she strolled with Henry around the hospital garden party, she could forget the days when she had to watch the proceedings from an upstairs window because the public must not be allowed to see her and her peers. Today's society may not be perfect, but would we have institutionalised Maria because of circumstances?

Henry was born in 1918, the sixth child in a family of ten. The family home was a three bed-roomed terrace house in a rural area - clean, but poorly furnished. The income was said to be adequate. His school life ended when he fell and broke his leg. During the fall he banged his head, and this was blamed for the onset of epilepsy. Following this incident, on his recovery, Henry was employed as a surface worker at a colliery - losing the job after a very short time on account of the frequency of his fits. He subsequently held various job for short periods of time only, due to the recurrent fits, but he did join the Armed Forces, where he received treatment for epilepsy in a Military Hospital before discharge. In 1935 his case was taken on board by a Health Visitor who paid quarterly visits to his home. At this time, his mother stated that Henry was excitable, with slow movements, and a tendency to masturbate excessively. Are any of these a crime severe enough to warrant certification? It would appear so, for shortly after the visits began, Henry was classified as border-line mentally defective - feeble-minded - and recommended for admission to an Institution. In 1949 he was reported by the Medical Superintendent of Highbury as being in need of certification under the Mental Deficiency Act of 1913. The petition was authorised in 1950, followed by representation by the parents for care and training for Henry in 1952. Was Henry becoming a nuisance at home? At this time both parents had retired, his father having been a miner, and although the income was adequate, pensions of 32 shillings and 6 pence (approx£1.63p) and 21 shillings and 6 pence (£1.13), they would not offer the care and supervision that Henry needed. There was also another son still living at home paying 45 shillings (£2.25p) for his board. The rent was 7shillings and 4 pence (37p) and they paid out 3 shillings 3 pence (17p) for insurance. Perhaps it would have been harsh to criticise Henry's parents; they were getting on in years and he must have been a burden at times. Yet how different might the life of Henry have been with recent methods of controlling epilepsy, and Government Training Schemes to fit him for the work of which he was so obviously capable.

As it was, Henry was employed in the Institution gardens, growing the vegetables and tending the animals which made it self-sufficient. He was not paid for his hard labour. When there was public outcry about exploitation, and it was deemed that the long hours of forced labour had to stop, even this job was lost to Henry. At first there was nothing to replace the work. Until the educational pursuits and social activities were introduced, a decade or so later, Henry, along with all the other residents, was left to spend the long days and evenings in idleness - surely a little exploitation was better than this. After all, in any 'normal' home there is work to be done, and the people who live there do it. For 27 years Henry had been a resident of Brentwood Ward, the male counter-part of Laurel Ward, - a light sentence, you may think. However Henry was still a reasonably young man when I returned to work at Highbury, so his sentence was to carry on. He was quite a pleasant, private person, the epileptic fits were few and far between, and he was extremely generous to the less able residents of both sexes, both with little gifts and, more importantly, with his time. He found an easy, affectionate relationship with Maria, and from the late 1960s onwards he enjoyed the use of his season ticket to the local second division football club. He shared light-hearted banter with most of the nursing staff, especially the females, and he always seemed quite contented with his lot, but I could not help but wonder why he was where he was.

In the mid I980s, Maria and Henry were moved into a Community Home run by the Social Services. They were kept together. It was a fairly small home, close to a shopping area, so Maria and Henry carried on pretty much as they had done during the more relaxed years in Highbury. They were very lucky compared to many of the elderly residents who left the hospital for other homes. They never did marry, but they spent the remaining years of their lives together in comfort, and as part of the wider community in the 'outside world'.

EMMA AND JOE

Have you ever witnessed the total adoration of one person for another, the complete giving of love, knowing that it is not returned in the same fullness? Such was the relationship between Emma and Joe. She worshipped him; she clung to him in every spare moment, so that she leaned physically toward him even when he was not there. Her frame was like the leaning tower of Pisa, one shoulder lower than the other from clinging in earnest adoration. It was sad that although they were 'courting' and together as much as possible, this worship was not appreciated or even returned.

Very little was known of Emma. She was born in 1909, and if her appearance when I first met her in the 1970s reflected that of days gone by, she must have been a great beauty in her youth. She had snow-white hair, naturally waved, framing a tanned face with brilliant blue eyes - the most beautiful eyes I had ever seen.

Emma attended a Special School, but was not a good scholar. In 1925, unable to get work, she was placed under the guardianship of an aunt. Sadly over the next few years she was found to be neglected, was certified as feeble-minded and despatched to an Institution in Derbyshire in 1935. She became an admission, a name with a diagnosis, for the records show little else.

This is a snap-shot of Emma. The picture does not do justice to her great beauty, nor does it show the brilliance of her bright blue eyes. Submissive and whimsical, the one great joy of Emma's life was her love for Joe, and the greatest pity was knowing that it was not returned in the same fullness.

In 1949 Emma was transferred to Highbury, and a social worker began the task of seeking relatives. In the meantime she performed menial jobs around the hospital, and always looked after her own person very well. Three years later a brother was found, but he might as well have stayed in obscurity for he refused any contact at all with Emma. He had 'no room for her', or 'time', and said that she must remain in the Hospital. In 1957 he was approached again regarding her discharge, and again he refused to help. Emma had nowhere else to go. Could we have expected him to help? By now Emma was 48 years old with 22 years of Institution life behind her, so would this brother have known anything about her? I believe that he could still have offered friendship if nothing else. Emma found some consolation in her love for Joe, albeit one-sided. Like Maria and Henry, they went out shopping and walking together, sat beside each other on the ward in the evenings when the sexes were finally allowed to mix, and strolled together on the outings organised for the unit. Joe ate her sweets, spent her money, and basked complacently in the adoration.

Joe was born in 1908, and like Emma was despatched to an Institution when he became of an age to work and was found to be without a job. He too had attended a Special School without much scholarly success, and so in 1925, at the age of 16, he was committed to Pewsey Poor Law Institution where he stayed until 1931. Transfer to a Southern Public Assistance Institution during this year was followed by a further transfer to the same Institution in Derbyshire where Emma was to become an inmate three years later, although in those times of the segregation of the sexes, they would have been unaware of each other.

Whilst in Derbyshire Joe was described as a good worker, spending long hours on the land, and was 'socially acceptable to the staff and other inmates'. Despite these favourable comments, there was yet another transfer to come in 1953....this time to Highbury. As with Emma, the diligent social workers made efforts to find relatives for Joe. In 1955 his father was found, and a visit was made to his home with a view to discharging Joe into his care. No mention of his mother had been made in any of the records since 1923, and it was found that Joe's father was now sharing a home with another woman. The house was described as situated in a working class locality, clean and adequately furnished. However, there was no chance of Joe being discharged to this home since his father's heart was failing, he was a dying man, and no-one could expect a female stranger to accept Joe.

So many of these accounts read alike: the crime of being poor, the well-used excuse of there being no room, the mothers who loved but died, the parents who were too old, the brothers and sisters who turned their backs on less fortunate siblings, and the tragedy of those who became forgotten. Joe could have gone home if there had been a home for him. As it was he had already spent thirty one years in some form of Institution, and was destined to spend another thirty years before he returned the outside community. For all his 'male chauvinism' towards Emma, Joe was a likeable fellow, extremely helpful and agile, even at the age of 66 when I met him for the first time. In the mid 1980s he and Emma were transferred to a home run by Mencap Homes Foundation, a little way from Highbury. Their courtship continued, but I cannot say exactly how much longer either of them lived because I myself left the area shortly afterwards.

WINNIE

1979 and Winnie had died. We, the nurses who had cared for her for so long, had stood helplessly beside her bed whilst she fought her battle with death. Her heart was not strong enough to withstand an amputation, so we had watched the gangrene creep steadily along her left leg - the lines on her wrinkled old face, once beautiful, deepened by the lingering pain she experienced. We had looked for some sign of the Winnie we had known so well - the Winnie with whom we had shared so many happy hours. All we could see was a wasting body, a parched mouth, a sweating brow....not a trace of our dear Winnie of a few weeks ago. Should you have entered Laurel Ward any time previously, you would almost certainly have been aware of a buxom old lady, weighed down by jewellery of all kinds - innumerable baubles, bangles, and beads. Her hair would have been curled, as it always was, by the use of the very old ‘dinky’ curlers, and she may have been grumbling about the tiniest of holes in her stocking. She had obviously been a very attractive woman in years gone by, and still did her best to maintain her appearance although she was approaching 82 years of age and was registered blind. Each night when she got into bed, she would laboriously twist her curlers into position, and she would have known every bead and brooch in her possession. This was Winnie!

Winnie was born in 1898 and came to Highbury in 1952 after passing through several other institutions. Her diagnosis was 'feeble-minded', but she was also classed as a Moral Defective. Her first encounter with Institution life came in 1931 when she was detained as 'needing a place of safety' in a Certified Institution in Lewes.

She was not blind in those days; she could read and write, and knew her age and personal history as well as anyone. Winnie's downfall came about because she liked male company, and already had three illegitimate children by different fathers at this time. With her curled hair and love of jewellery and make-up, present even then, Winnie must have been quite a woman!

Even in the late 1970s it was difficult to persuade many of our residents to use make-up, especially to have 'red lips', because they were born in an era when only 'loose women' carried on in this way. Accepting this as a fact, it is easy to see how Winnie must have looked to her accusers.

Following her admission to Lewes, there is a gap in the records, for the next we know is that the Commissioners of the Board of Control visited Cuckfield Public Assistance Institution and ordered Winnie to be certified as a Mental Defective. It was recorded that at this time she would only work under supervision, although she had held a job in domestic service for many years prior to admission. On all early reports there was always great emphasis placed upon how much work an 'inmate-to-be' could do and how well they could do it. Maybe there was something in the idea of 'cheap labour' which helped to revolutionise the Institutional system many decades later.

Winnie was detained 'for her own safety and for that of others' - it being stated that she had to be 'led away from men' because of her unnatural attitude towards them. She stayed at Cuckfield, it can be assumed from the records, until her transfer to Highbury. In 1952 one of Winnie's daughters took her home on licence: this entailed being totally responsible for Winnie under the supervision of a social worker who visited the home at regular intervals to assess the situation.

If home conditions were satisfactory, the social worker submitted completed forms to the Medical Officer in charge of the inmate concerned to verify the fact. The forms contained details of the composition of the household, the state of the house (i.e. clean or dirty), income and expenditure, and answered the obvious question, 'Is everything being done to prevent procreation?' By now Winnie was 54 years old!!

In Winnie's case the home conditions were excellent, but the daughter was reluctant to accept total care of her mother since this was a person whom she barely knew. Thus, although the social worker recommended several extensions to the licence, which could have led to eventual release, life dealt a further blow to Winnie, and her detention continued. What happened to Winnie's other children is unknown, but this particular daughter, even though I had never seen her visit the hospital (except for the funeral), had always remembered to send cards at Easter, Christmas, Mother's Day, and of course on Winnie's birthday. Surprisingly Winnie always knew when these occasions were due, despite so many long years in care, and with every day the same as the one before. Until almost the end of her life, Winnie was a very lively, robust old lady; she loved her food! Her habits were scrupulously clean, and her accent was decidedly 'posh'. Arthritis in her knees hampered her walking, but other than this Winnie was a remarkable, attractive eighty-one year-old. Latent diabetes robbed her of her sight, and eventually brought about the gangrene, but prior to that Winnie had been a very fit woman.

A favourite time of mine on the ward was the quiet period following lunch, when most of the staff had retired for their lunch breaks, and those of us who were left could relax with the residents, and give a little extra attention to each one. At such a time, when she was alive, Winnie was the centre of attraction. Being blind, and hard of hearing, happy with her own thoughts, she tended to be unconsciously neglected in the bustle of the day, but in the quiet time she blossomed. She was given objects to feel, to shake, to smell, and if possible to recognise. Seldom was she wrong. If given a bottle of perfume, she would, like the grand, sophisticated old lady she was, pretend to tip the contents and dab behind each ear, breathing in the imaginary scent. On one occasion someone passed Winnie a packet of cigarettes. Instinct told her that pressure must be gentle to protect the package. Carefully she opened the pack and took out a cigarette. In her beautifully refined voice she informed the nurses present that she used to smoke - sin of sins in her day. We found an ash-tray, let her feel it upon her lap, and placed a lighted cigarette between her lips. She puffed away like a habitual smoker, and promptly snapped her fingers to demand a glass of wine. We always kept a bottle of sherry in the cupboard - it was useful with beaten eggs if an elderly resident was sick or not eating well - and so Winnie's request was granted. She sat in regal elegance, her cigarette in one hand and her sherry in the other, her past memories flowing from her lips like poetry. For a few brief seconds of time Winnie transformed the ward, which had long been her home, into a royal court.

How different would Winnie's life have been if she had been born in today's society - a society where, whatever our own personal views, the pill and abortion are freely available. She could have enjoyed her love of male company without reproach or even a side-ways glance. Some might say that the young of today are very lucky - they are allowed to retain their freedom, whilst Winnie paid dearly for her folly. She was in her mid 30s before she was compulsorily detained, so, in comparison to many of our residents, hers had been a light sentence. Yet I always felt a touch of sadness that such dignity and sophistication should have been hidden away behind locked doors for half a century.

In terms of records and documentation, there was precious little to write about Winnie's life - but for the sparse account of her eventual detention, she might never have existed at all. However, she was a wonderful character, who managed to be her own person through 48 years of being in care, and for that reason she deserves a few pages in a book. It is unlikely I shall ever encounter another Winnie, and so I think myself very lucky to have known this one.

ADA AND EDIE

Otherwise known as Tweedle-dum and Tweedle-dee, these two old ladies were as alike as two peas in a pod. Inseparable throughout their time in Highbury, they were able to teach us all the true meaning of the word friendship.

Each year, early in the season, approximately fifty of our residents would spend a week at a holiday camp on the east coast, where a few weeks of every year were reserved for the Mentally Handicapped. Our residents would be amongst others from hospitals throughout the country, and would appear to be a bunch of old folk enjoying the sea-side, in comparison to many of the others who were much younger and sometimes physically handicapped as well.

This type of holiday was well organised, with entertainment, bars, and fancy dress competitions, but many of our residents preferred their second holiday of the year - self-catering in chalets near Great Yarmouth - because of the more relaxed atmosphere. I have shared a self-catering holiday with them, and enjoyed myself as much as they did - jacket potatoes at midnight, wine with dinner at 10.30p.m., leisurely breakfasts and no time schedule to keep. How different from hospital life, and indeed the holiday camp, where even the meal- times had to be routine on account of the great numbers to be fed! Nevertheless, the staff at the camp were very kind to the holiday-makers, making special efforts to meet the needs of the Mentally Handicapped. The highlight of the week to some of our old folk was the fancy dress parade, and we seldom left without prizes. One particular year two ladies from Laurel Ward, Ada and Edie, entered the competition as Tweedle-dum and Tweedle-dee. So much did they look the part that they were often referred to by these names. Both stood 4ft 8 inches high, with chubby little bodies on chubby little legs. Both had snow-white hair, and the stooped back of the elderly, robbing them of a few inches. Ada had a round, happy face, while Edie was as wrinkled as a muffin and looked remarkably like a garden gnome.

Ada was born in 1906 and came to Highbury in 1949 — another diagnosis of being ‘feeble-minded’. She spent her child-hood with her parents, one brother and one sister, and was described at school as being ‘unable to learn’. In 1924, aged 18, she was admitted to a Poor Law Institution - she could not earn a living and was literally destitute. From the Poor Law Institution she was transferred to a Certified Institution for Mental Defectives in Derbyshire, and finally in 1949 she came to Highbury.

Ada’s father died shortly after her arrival there, and her mother went to live with her daughter, Ada’s sister. When, in 1958, along with all other Mental Defectives, Ada was de-certified and release was considered, this sister was approached regarding the future of her care. As the sister had three children, and her mother living with her, she refused to give Ada a home. Nor would Ada’s mother become totally responsible for her welfare, giving the same reason - lack of space. How familiar became the reasons! Too old; lack of space; being strangers to their own kin; poor income, and the all-too-often heard, ‘they are so much better off where they are’.

This is all we knew of Ada in 1974. It would appear that there had been nothing else of importance to record in this 68 year long life. She was truly a forgotten person. As far as society was concerned, Ada’s life has been summed up in fewer than one hundred words, simply because her parents could not support her and she could not support herself.

Edie was born in 1897, and was despatched to Highbury in 1928, diagnosed as feeble-minded. Like her friend Ada, she spent her childhood with her parents. She was one of a large family, several siblings dying at birth or in infancy, and there remained alive in 1974 three sisters and Edie herself. According to the early records, it was deemed that the whole family was of weak intellect. Edie attended school until she was l4yrs old but did not learn a great deal, and was therefore incapable of earning a living when she left.

Her father had no fixed occupation, and both parents drank heavily, using any money available for this purpose. Edie had two illegitimate children by different fathers, and they too lived with her and her parents. On January 5th 1928 Edie was reported by the Board of Control as having served one month's hard labour in prison for neglecting her children, a girl aged six and a boy aged two and a half. One month of hard labour! Would that happen today? Perhaps here is one instance where our society of today could take example from the past. What happens nowadays to our child-neglecters and baby- batterers? So often we reprimand, but look for reasons, and so often return the victim to the same cruelty following a promise of 'It won't happen again', How many times does it happen again, sometimes with tragic results? Yes, I believe that we could learn from Edie's experience.

Because Edie was living with her parents, they served a lighter six-month sentence for allowing the neglect. On her release from prison, Edie was admitted to Highbury as a place of safety. At this time the hospital was a Poor Law Institution, and the victims of the cruelty - the two maltreated children - were also placed in different Institutions of the same kind. We knew that Edie's daughter still remained 'inside' in 1974, but nothing more was ever known about her son. Introduced many years later by a diligent social worker, mother and daughter became firm friends and exchanged letters (Edie's being written by a nurse) and the occasional visits. Elsie was a mirror image of her mother, but she was quite a few inches taller.

There is a long gap in Edie's records following her admission in 1928, for the next date we saw was 1955; twenty-seven years and nothing eventful to be remembered? Probably twenty-seven years of hard graft for a pittance! Not worth a mention! Make up for it in 1955! It was suggested in this year that Edie's married sister be given occasional care of her. However, she was already caring for a second sister, on licence from a Mental Defective Colony (awful words) since their mother had died. On visiting this sister, a divorcee, it was ascertained that she lived in a very clean cottage which she owned. She was in receipt of £2 from her ex-husband, and a little extra for sub-letting her garage. She had one married daughter. Conditions were good for licence for Edie, but in October 1955, her sister refused to help because she already had one Mentally Handicapped sister in her care. This second sister, the very lucky one, was de-certified in 1958, as was Edie, and was released to live a normal life in the outside world — no longer to be bothered by the Authorities.

Alas for Edie, she was not so fortunate. She was destined to spend another twenty-five years in care, making a total of fifty-two altogether, before she left the hospital to live elsewhere.

In 1980 Edie and Ada were moved into a large, privately owned Residential Home - by this time Edie was 83 yrs old and Ada was approaching 75. The only blessing was that they were moved together, for they had always been inseparable. Other than that, nothing good came of the move - it had come too late! Edie and Ada got lost among the other fifty or so residents of the home. They lost the intimacy of the hospital ward where they had lived for so long, and it is surprising that they both survived for another two years. On visits to see them after the move, I never felt that they were happy, and I always left the home wondering if Edie and Ada had thought that I had gone to fetch them 'home', or even that I had betrayed them. I hope they knew that those decisions weren't mine.

Edie's daughter spent the same fifty-two years in care as did her mother, and then she herself was moved from the hospital where she had lived into a half-way house, a home between hospital and community life. She had learned to read and write, to add figures and basic cookery and cleaning, and so hopefully she had a better quality of life in her later years. If she is still alive today, she will be 80 years old.

BRENTWOOD WARD

The Mental Health Department, as it was known in 1974, was made up of three wards. The three wards were called after trees, Laurel, Hazel, and Brentwood. Laurel and Hazel housed females, and Brentwood housed the male residents. In the 1980s, as the elderly men and women were moved into the community or died, purpose-built units replaced the old workhouse buildings to accommodate the younger generation of mentally and physically handicapped who filled their places. By this time the males and females were living together, whereas in the years before it was strictly taboo!

With the exception of one or two, the men of Brentwood Ward were gentlemen in the true sense of the word - courteous, respectful and mostly full of fun, despite long years spent in Institutions. Ernest, Arthur, William and Tommy were four of these gentlemen for whom I had great affection. Ernest was born in 1907 and came to Highbury in 1950, yet another feeble-minded person. He attended a special school followed by a period at another school where trades were taught. According to the old records, Ernest did not benefit from either. Upon leaving, however, he did hold down a job as a parks labourer.

On April 13th 1927 Ernest's mother was appointed as his guardian - a better option for Ernest than being sent to an Institution, although he was still certified under the Mental Defective Act 1913. He had been sadly neglected and this was a way of keeping an eye on him. The guardianship was extended five yearly until a varying order to send him to an Institution was filed in 1950 following his mother's death. Thus Ernest came to Highbury Hospital, aged 43.

Throughout the records there is no mention of Ernest's father, but in 1952 his half-sister was approached regarding her taking over from his mother. She chose to leave Ernest where he was, and since there were no other relatives to ask, Ernest was still with us in 1974. He was a well-dressed old gentleman, doing his share of light domestic work on the ward, which must have seemed like paradise to him for the men also worked shifts in the hospital laundry, and tilled the land to provide food for the inmates in the Institution days. He could now relax in his twilight years, but what a lot of living he had missed!

We, the nursing staff, did our best to recapture a little of that lost living by organising day trips and evenings out. On one such occasion my husband and I took nine residents in a minibus to the Goose Fair and Ernest was one of the party. It was a very cold wet evening in October but since none of our passengers had ever seen the fairground by night, we trudged around in the mud. When eyes stopped popping at the magnificent lights, and all the 'oohs' and 'ahhs' had been said, we decided to round off our evening in the warm lounge of the local pub. Remember that our passengers were all elderly people feeling the excitement that we had felt as children, and we were reluctant for this evening of magic to come to an end. Into the pub we streamed, soaking wet and bedraggled, but radiating the pleasure we all felt inside. The first round of drinks disappeared, and Ernest tipped his glass like a hardened drinker, savouring every drop. I knew that he wasn't taking any form of medication, nor were the others, so the glasses were refilled a second, third, and fourth time. Crisps, peanuts, and pork scratchings were eaten with gusto, and we left the pub at closing time along with all the regulars. Alas, this was remembered as the night that Ernest lost his teeth! His bottom set of dentures dropped into the toilet on his return to the ward, and in his tired happiness Ernest bade them goodbye as he joyfully flushed them away. Evenings such as this could never erase the years of emptiness that had gone before for Ernest and the other residents, but they could ensure that the years to come would hold affection and companionship for a great many elderly folk like Ernest and his very dear friend Arthur.

Arthur was born 1909, and came to Highbury in 1948, after 'doing the rounds' of several other Institutions. His first admission had been brought about by notification from the Local Education Authority upon his reaching his sixteenth birthday. Again, a case of not having a job! In 1922 Arthur had been attending a Special school in Derbyshire, but upon leaving he was to begin the well-trodden journey around Institution corridors. His final report from school in 1925 stated that he was capable of learning manual work, and his own doctor had long been urging his parents to place Arthur into an institution to give him a chance to fulfil this.

Whilst at school Arthur had spent most of his time working with a cobbler, a task which he enjoyed and did well. Why wasn't this aptitude for cobbling encouraged? I asked myself. The report also stated that Arthur had an exceptional memory, and this remained true throughout his life. If you were to ask Arthur what day of the week was May 7th 1963 (or any other date), after a few quick mumbles he would tell you, and he was always right.

Arthur had a good, living father, a horse-man earning 36 shillings (approx £1.8O) per week plus house, milk and potatoes. He was anxious about his son, but because he had four other children less than thirteen years old, and the fact that he was struggling to make ends meet, he offered to pay 2 shillings (l0p) per week towards Arthur's care in an institution; the year was 1925.

Arthur was certified as an imbecile with a mental age of eight, and was removed to a Staffordshire Poorhouse. A subsequent home visit in 1932 revealed a clean home, but an overcrowded one, lacking the supervision that Arthur was said to need. In simple words, there was no room for him. In any case, the Visitors of Institutions for Defectives maintained at that time that Arthur was unfit to return home — he could not add up figures and could only write simple words. He was transferred to a second institution in 1933, and on to a Public Assistance Institution in 1935. By the end of 1935 he could read, do simple additions, and knew his multiplications up to the eight times table. He had progressed from being an imbecile, but not until 1947 was his diagnosis changed to feeble-minded.

Home conditions were reviewed again, and still found to be unsuitable, though reasons were not given on this occasion. So it was that in 1947 Arthur arrived at Highbury, the building that was to become his resting place for many years, despite a further attempt to secure his discharge in 1952. During this year the home situation was assessed again. Father had died; mother, now aged 56, was employed as a domestic earning £1 per week plus widow's pension of 10 shillings (50p). A sixteen-year-old daughter was still living at home and bringing in the sum of £2. 10 shillings (£2.50) per week for land work. Rent was 5 shillings and 6 pence (approx 28p) and the rates were £2. 10 shillings (£2.46) half-yearly. This situation did not appear too bad financially, but again Arthur was refused discharge on the grounds of insufficient supervision. This could have been Arthur's chance!

Hope for Arthur was becoming non-existent, but the hospital managers were not easily deterred in his case and made a fourth attempt to release him in 1957: so many attempts and all fruitless. Yet the attempts alone are enough to prove that Arthur was capable of an ordinary existence. By 1957 his mother lived alone, her family all having families of their own. She was in receipt of 32shillings and sixpence (£1.63) widow's pension plus 8shillings (4Op) per week National Assistance. Rent and rates were the same as in 1952, and mother had ceased to work, which meant supervision was now available. Why then was Arthur still with us in 1974? Simply because his mother did not want him, and she said so!

Arthur's brothers and sisters never came to visit him at Highbury— had they forgotten that he ever existed? We were his only family; we watched him as he tended the tomatoes in the green-house in the small garden attached to Brentwood Ward, and we grieved for the blow he had been dealt by fate. Arthur always seemed to be contented enough, but his eyes lacked the lustre of a man with a purpose.

Try this one on your friends: if three men sat in a row, Jim to the right of Tom, and Tom to the right of Harry, who would be in the middle? It looks simple written down, doesn't it, but imagine it being asked of a man who was diagnosed as feeble-minded and slow at answering questions. This is what happened to Alfred, who in 1974 was a polite, well-dressed, well-spoken gentleman residing on Brentwood Ward.

Alfred was born in 1919, attended a church school until he was eight years old, and then went on to a private school. He could read and write and did odd jobs for his mother in all of his spare time. In 1936 a health visitor called on Alfred and his widowed mum, for he had reached and passed the age of employment without having a paid job. Subsequent quarterly visits followed and the usual reports were filed. How would Alfred fare as a result of these reports?

Alfred was described as slow and uncertain, shy and reticent, quiet and well-conducted. In 1938 his G.P. suggested the need for care and training, and the following year Alfred's mother made representation to the Local Authority for this purpose. A petition was signed appointing her as Alfred's guardian, after a medical examination had led to his being certified as feeble-minded. This was 1939 and home conditions were very good. Alfred lived with his mum in a five- roomed cottage in the country, very clean, and the income consisted of 10shillings (50p) per week widow's pension, plus 6 shillings and 9 pence (35p), which was a disability pension. Rent and rates worked out at 5shillings 4 pence (27p).

Alfred's mother exercised constant supervision, and the Guardianship was renewed at two yearly intervals until she died in 1949. At this time no other relative, or any other person, could be found who would perform the duty of parent to Alfred. He was removed to Highbury. It must be stated here that the psychiatrist in charge at the time really tried to find a 'replacement mum'. It must also be noted that Alfred's diagnosis changed in that year - he had now become an imbecile, hard to believe, knowing the Alfred of many years later.

In 1950 an aunt of his was found by a very conscientious social worker. The aunt could provide adequate supervision and also had room to accommodate Alfred, so he was allowed a holiday of one week, on licence, at her home. She would not however accept total responsibility for him, and so Alfred had to be content with visiting her on alternate Sundays. These visits continued until she died, and then Alfred was alone, but lucky to be still young enough and fit enough to benefit from the new freedom to be found in hospital units of our kind over the next two decades.

Alfred was a particular favourite of mine; he was a gentleman to whom I often referred with affection as our 'professional mourner'. When any other resident died Alfred would ask to attend the funeral - he knew the service by heart. His words were clear and well-spoken, with great reverence for the departed. Since his address in the 1930s was that of a vicarage, and he had attended a church school, I am convinced that he was the son of a parson. No mention was made in the early records of his father; indeed, Alfred himself never spoke of him, but Alfred was certainly well versed in the scriptures.

Even in 1949 when Alfred first arrived at Highbury, great emphasis was placed on church or chapel attendance, but Alfred's religious knowledge was far superior to that of anyone else. Long after church and chapel attendance was relaxed, and the residents were given the choice of whether they wished to attend or give it a miss, Alfred continued to worship twice every Sunday. In fact, most of the residents continued to attend the services, sometimes with great difficulty due to age and disability, and the fact that the services were held in an upstairs room which served as a church. For many it was a case of 'old habits die hard', and they had spent so many years being told that they must go!

In the mass exodus of the long-stay residents in the 1980s, Arthur, Ernest, and Alfred were transferred to the same residential home run by the local Social Services.

Arthur was 71 years old, Ernest was 73, and Alfred was a mere 61 year old. I cannot say when any of them died, but I am aware that all of them spent a few happy years living in the home, and were totally accepted by the local community. Who would not accept three such lovely old gentlemen?

The following page shows a copy of the form used to allow an inmate to be absent from the Institution, or removed temporarily from the care of his/her appointed Guardian e.g. in the case of Alfred, for whom guardianship was given to the Medical Superintendent of the hospital upon the death of his mother, and who was allowed absence for a week's holiday with his aunt. The form was signed and duly dated by the County Medical Officer once the agreement was reached to allow absence.

What fantastic progress was made since a form such as this was completed for Alfred in 1950! Two decades later, a few words with a doctor, simple transport arrangements and our younger residents could have spent holidays on the moon if it were possible and of course if it was to their benefit. Who, in those early years, could have envisaged our older residents, and the younger ones who followed them, taking trips to France or being able to choose where they would like to go, and more importantly, what they would like to do when they got there?

....COUNTY COUNCIL, MENTAL DEFICIENCY ACTS.

Mental Deficiency Regulations 1948, Article n.o.70

Permitting a patient to be absent from the care of the appointed guardian.

To:...

In pursuance of the power conferred by the above mentioned Acts and the

Regulations made thereunder, consent is hereby given to...................being absent

From the care of............................of............................the appointed guardians,

the period from.........................to..........................on the following conditions:-

1. The said patient shall be under your personal care and control and shall not reside elsewhere than with you except with the written permission of the Local Health Authority.
2. The said patient shall forthwith be returned to the appointed guardian on ....or at an earlier date upon the written request of the Local Health Authority.
3. The said patient shall at all times receive adequate care and supervision (N.B. Special attention is called to the necessity for preventing defectives from forming attachments with the opposite sex, and any inclination to do so must be reported at once to me.)
4. That full access to the said patient shall at all times be afforded to any officer of the Board of Control or of the.............................Local Health Authority duly authorised for the purpose of ascertaining the condition and progress of the said patient.

....

County Medical Officer.

DATE..

An afternoon in the sun! Sitting on the bench from left to right: Ada, Ronnie (Monkey as we knew him), Maurice and Edie. If you look closely you will see that Monkey is knitting - see the tassels on his latest long scarf? The knitting needles were never out of his hands. You can see the resemblance between Ada and Edie - is there any wonder that we referred to them as Tweedle-dum and Tweedle-dee? They were inseparable, went everywhere together, despite Edie sometimes being quite nasty to Ada. Maurice is not mentioned in the book - he was a comparative new-corner to Highbury, but he was Edie's boyfriend although he was a good 30 years younger than her. He escorted her to dances and to the films, but he couldn't replace Ada as Edie's closest friend.

RONNIE AND DENNIS

I met Ronnie for the first time in 1972. Highbury Hospital was desperately short of trained nurses, and was advertising in the local papers for anyone who could help, allowing great flexibility with working hours. Having left the N.H.S. in 1966 to start a family, and in 1972 being the mother of two young children, it was difficult for me to do very much. However, I did offer my services, and started work on a short- term part-time contract. I was employed as a relief Staff Nurse, and thus covered any area where a trained nurse was needed. I spent most of my six months working on Brentwood Ward, and it was there that I met Ronnie — short, stocky, weathered and wrinkled, with his mouth always curved in a half- smile, and his mop of dark hair always unkempt.

I knew very little about him: when he introduced himself he said his name was Monkey and he had been born in Bristol Zoo six-hundred years ago! His accent was certainly Bristolian, and I found out that he had been transferred to Highbury from an Institution in the South-west of England. Monkey's great passion was knitting - a great fan of Notts Forest FC., his speciality was knitting long, very long, red and white scarves. On one occasion, contractors were working on Brentwood Ward, and Monkey kindly offered to look after the hand-knitted jumper of one of the plumbers. During the day he found a loose end in the wool, and wound the jumper into balls. At the end of the day he returned the garment to the workman, but it wasn't a jumper anymore! The plumber had become the proud owner of two beautifully knitted long scarves! Fortunately he had a sense of humour, and accepted the scarves gracefully. From that day until the work was completed, the plumber arrived to work wearing a leather jacket!

Monkey was still on Brentwood Ward when I returned to the hospital in full-time work in 1974. He continued to insist that he was born in Bristol Zoo, and declared that he was now eight-hundred years old! His passion for knitting football scarves had not diminished, and my son, still has today, a long black and white Notts County scarf, knitted as a special favour for me all those years ago. I deemed it quite an honour, considering that Monkey was a supporter of Notts Forest, and indeed held a season ticket for that club, along with five other gentlemen residents of Brentwood Ward.

Sadly Monkey died as a result of stomach cancer only two years after I had returned to work. His presence on the ward, and his friendly chatter was sorely missed. Until his final days, Monkey's temperament had never changed - always a smile, a joke, a pleasant word, and the inevitable furious working of his fingers as his knitting needles click-clicked to the end of yet another scarf.

So little had been known about Monkey's life before Highbury - it was almost as if he had suddenly become a person on the day of his transfer from a previous Institution. However, he is even now remembered by those of us who knew him, and his cheeky ways will stay in my memory forever. Each time Notts County is mentioned on the radio, the T.V. or in the papers, the black and white scarf comes to mind, and his wrinkled, weathered face comes with it.

Another face which stays with me is the gaunt and haunted look of Dennis, medium height, skinny, slouched and slightly slovenly in appearance, his dark sad eyes expressionless. Originally from Ireland, Dennis was not popular amongst his peers. In fact, he was very unpopular - he told tales, 'snitched' on his fellow residents, sometimes lying if need be.

Dennis failed miserably in trying to gain favour with the nursing and domestic staff, and I recall that he never had a friend in all the time I knew him. Dennis was a loner! He was a man it would have been easy to dislike, but from somewhere deep within me I found a soft spot for him - a sad and lonely childhood had left a sad and lonely adult. Abandoned in an Institution by parents who simply did not want him had left Dennis in search of love for the rest of his life. He didn't know how to make friends - how could one who had never known love give love? Sadly, because of the length of time he had spent institutionalised, Dennis had become a forgotten cause.

He never forgot his Irish roots. St. Patrick's Day was etched in his memory, and he once confided that he would like shamrock for a button-hole. We had shamrock growing in our garden, and I filled a plant pot with the seed pods for him. Unfortunately it did not bloom that particular year, but Dennis nurtured the plant as a mother would a child, and he was amply rewarded the following year. A simple gift, maybe the only act of kindness he had ever been shown, and until his dying day, Dennis remembered that gift and the bearer of it. He died in the 1980s from bowel cancer. I cannot remember the exact year, but I do remember hoping at the time that Dennis found the love he so craved in another place.

As with so many of our residents in those days, the nursing and domestic staff were the only mourners at the funeral of Dennis. An area set aside from the main burial area of a cemetery in Nottingham was the last resting place for so many of our old people, and there they lie - forgotten in death as they were forgotten in life.

There were so many 'characters' among the men of Brentwood Ward that it would be impossible to mention every one, but Tommy has to be worth a line or two.

Regardless of the weather, you would have seen him almost running around the hospital grounds, a little old man, resembling a leprechaun and looking as if he could disappear quite easily before your eyes. His bald head and withered features were weather-worn, but you would have been entranced by the twinkle in his old eyes, like sunshine dancing upon an ocean. This was Tommy, and one glimpse of him would make you think of mischief on two legs.

He was born in 1896, and came to Highbury in 1950 diagnosed as feeble-minded. He could read and write, having attended school until he was fourteen years old. On leaving school he was employed as a farm labourer earning 12 shillings and sixpence (approx 63p), but he would only work under supervision — how familiar that sounds! When a health visitor called at his home in 1934, he was found to be out of work and without visible means of support. The inevitable quarterly visits ensued, and on one such visit Tommy was accused of frightening women and young girls at night. Even in 1974 when I first met Tommy, aged78, he still had an eye for the pretty nurses, and it could be said that he possessed a certain charisma, for all the staff were affectionately drawn towards him.

The next date (there had been nothing since 1934) to be mentioned in Tommy's records was 1948 following his admission to the County Institution. His mother had died and Tommy's brother consented to his detention. Prior to this there had been no recorded details about Tommy's family. From the Institution he was transferred to

Highbury in 1950. He was de-certified in 1958, but by then there was no home to which he could be discharged. Those few lines have summed up Tommy's life as far as society was concerned, and he was one person who was destined to live out his life in the hospital. He was our own magical little sprite, tormenting the ladies until the day he died at the age of 84 in 1980. Tommy was sadly missed by everyone, and I like to think that he is sitting under a shamrock somewhere mending shoes.

LAUREL WARD

The lay-out of Laurel ward has been described earlier within these pages. This ward was my area of responsibility, along with one staff nurse, three enrolled nurses, five auxiliary nurses, and a team of domestic staff which included three orderlies who took care of the kitchen area. No words could describe the efficiency of the team of staff on Laurel ward. A mention must also be made of the work done by those nurses on the night shift who carried on with social activities long after we on day duty had left to go home.

Hilda was born in 1906. She came from a good home, where her father was a hosiery hand with an income of £3 per week. Her mother had died when Hilda was three years old, and her father had re-married. His second wife produced three children, and she had little time for the child of the first marriage. She considered the child, our Hilda, to be 'backward'. Granted the child's educational attainments were low, even though she had attended school, but were they so poor that she could not be looked after at home? It seems that they were, for in 1918 Hilda's father committed her to care in a home for children in Cardiff. Since childhood swiftly passes and Hilda was already 12 years old, she could not be expected to stay at the home for long; then began her tour of Institutions.

From 1923-1933 she was an inmate of a Southern Poor Law Institution; from 1933-1935, an inmate of a Midland Public Assistance Institution, and in 1935, she arrived at Highbury - not yet a hospital, but an Institution for Defectives. When I arrived at Highbury in 1974, Hilda was 68 years old and had already spent fifty-seven years of her life 'in care', with little else to record other than her transferrals from one place to another. I found Hilda to be a clean, well-spoken old lady who loved 'nice hair-do's' and enjoyed pottering around the ward doing little jobs. True, she was a trifle childish and simple-minded, but what opportunity did she have to develop intellectually while spending so many years shut away from society? Would she have been different if her mother had lived, or if her stepmother had not been the kind we recognise in fairy stories from our own childhood? Knowing Hilda as I did, seeing her caring for herself and for her possessions, helping her peers, it is hard not to believe that she could have been helped at sometime during those forgotten years. What kind of society allows the young to be so ill-used that they are like unwanted baggage, moved from storage place to storage place?

Hilda was moved into a home run by Mencap Homes Foundation in the 1980s and lived out the rest of her life quite happily along with others, male and female, who had shared her experiences in various Institutions.

Lizzie was another old lady who should not have spent so long in care. In 1950 she was admitted to Highbury for the second time. She was born in 1905, attended elementary school, and was engaged in domestic service for a few years. Unfortunately in 1933 Lizzie became pregnant and entered Highbury - which at that time was a County Institution - for the first time. Home conditions were found to be unsuitable, and the Relieving Officer committed her to care. Lizzie's son was born in the Institution, and stayed with her until he was aged seven, and was then put up for adoption. He was one of the lucky ones who did find a family willing to take care of him, but although he knew of his mother and her whereabouts, he avoided any close contact. He used to make twice-yearly phone calls to ask after her health, and these were, very infrequently, followed by a visit, or so I was told! In 14 years spent working at Highbury, I never saw him.

In 1948 Lizzie was discharged by the House Visiting Sub-committee into a Nottinghamshire Residential Establishment. Attempts were made to discharge her into society, but there was nowhere for her to go, and Lizzie was re-admitted to Highbury in 1950— still diagnosed as feeble-minded, just as she had been at the time of her pregnancy fifteen years earlier.

When I met Lizzie in 1974, she had already spent forty-one years 'in captivity'. She was a very attractive 69 year old, scrupulously clean in her habits and caring lovingly for her possessions, which in former years had been non-existent. She tended to save her money, but when she did spend she did so wisely. She enjoyed music and dancing, and belonged to an O.A.P. club in the local town. Lizzie was by nature a happy person, content with her lot, and this helped to make her a popular addition to the Residential Home into which she moved in 1983.

Most of our residents at Highbury were very active old people looking much younger than they were, and trotting about like men and women of middle age. One such lady was Harriet, diagnosed as feeble-minded in 1937, unable to read or write, and lacking any comprehension of money ....or so they said! From the day I started working at the hospital, Harriet took it upon herself to shop for almost every member of staff, and could be trusted to buy several items from different shops and always return with the correct change. If she was one penny short she could check the goods, decide where she had been 'robbed', and promptly return to collect her dues. Lacking comprehension of money? I think not! She loved the feeling of being trusted to shop for us, and very often when we didn't really want anything, someone would come up with something for Harriet to go and buy.

Harriet was born in 1911, attended school until she was nearly twelve, and held several menial situations doing light domestic work after she had left. During these years she lived with her mother, father and one brother - her sisters being married and having homes of their own. The home was clean but poor; father was getting 10 shillings (50p) old age pension, 5 shillings (25p) from Public Assistance, and this was supplemented by £1 for board and lodgings from her brother who worked as a labourer. Harriet did not do well at her jobs, and even in later years could remember how her mother warned her about being headstrong, and telling her 'where she would end up!' Threats of the Workhouse were not uncommon in those days - most of our residents, and older nursing staff who had retired and still visited the hospital, recalled having heard those words.
It is not surprising to learn that Harriet became unemployed, and came to the attention of the Local Authority via the Unemployment Assistance Board in 1937. With the guidance of her own G.P. it was decided that Harriet would benefit both physically and mentally if she was removed from her parents' home. In that same year she became an inmate of a certified Institution in Derbyshire. Harriet did improve, and was allowed, on licence, to spend holidays with her former Sunday School teacher.

These holidays continued even after Harriet's transferral to Highbury in 1949, but by the time I met Harriet in 1974, they had ceased due to the age of her friend. Communication by then was limited to letters (read to Harriet by nursing staff) and very rare visits. Harriet's sisters also visited occasionally, but preferred to send letters containing money. I often suggested that a nurse could take Harriet to visit one of her sister's homes, but this was always met with cold disapproval from the relatives. However, after such a suggestion, there was always an extra letter and also an extra £1! Harriet made sure that the letters were answered almost immediately to ensure her next 'windfall'.

In 1975 Harriet was interviewed by a consultant psychiatrist, and he asked her if she knew when she had come to Highbury. She answered with the exact day, date, year, and even added the time for good measure. Then, with a smile like that of a cat who had had the cream, Harriet also gave the exact time, day, date, and year of her original admission to the Institution in Derbyshire. The psychiatrist's first response was to wonder why she was still in care whilst capable of such accuracy. He then asked what I was doing on June 3rd 1949 at 2p.m. Needless to say I couldn't remember; I supposed I must have been at school.

Each time the anniversary of Harriet's admission came around, she would add on another year, and insist that she would only leave 'in her box'. Harriet didn't leave in her box — she was moved into a community home run by the Social Services, and the last I heard of her was that she was often seen running around the City centre of Nottingham, shopping for her carers; not bad for a 73 year old woman who was diagnosed as feeble-minded at the age of 26, some forty-seven years earlier!

In one paragraph I am going to tell you about Lottie. She was diagnosed as feeble-minded in 1942, and came to Highbury in 1949. She was born in 1914 and lived with her mother, father, and one brother in a clean, but poorly furnished home. Father was a brass bobbin finisher and mother was a housewife, getting a little help from Lottie, who although she had attended a Special school, was “slow of words and deeds”. Mother and father cared for her, and not until mother died was Lottie certified and prepared for ‘removal’ to Highbury. This had to happen, for Lottie’s father could not give up working to exercise the care and supervision which had been available while Lottie’s mum was alive. In those few words you have read the summary of a life-time, for although there were occasional postcards from Lottie’s brother, she never saw him again. Lottie was one of our residents who could not cope with the transition from hospital to a Community Home, and she died within a few weeks of her move.

Eva was born in 1903. She never attended a school of any kind, and lived with her father and sister in a very clean, but inadequately furnished home. No mention is made of her mother in any of the records. Although the sister was a hard-working woman, Eva’s father, a miner, was more out of work than in work, and Eva herself was never gainfully employed. She was in receipt of outdoor relief from June 1922 until she was admitted to the County Institution in 1930 for the birth of her illegitimate son. The child was maintained in various homes following his birth, but somewhere along the line he got lost in the system, and in later years no-one could find a trace of his whereabouts.

After the confinement, Eva was transferred to a residential establishment and then returned to the Institution - now known as Highbury - in 1950. She could not return to the family home: her father was ill, and her sister was getting older. During the 1970s Eva helped in the launderette of Laurel Ward, vastly different from the Institution laundry work she had done in the past. With our modern washing machines and dryers she could almost relax while she worked, doing only personal linen - no longer the sheets and blankets of the early days. For one diagnosed as feeble-minded, Eva's vocabulary was amazing, and her understanding of modern-day equipment was astounding. She adapted to decimalisation quicker than anyone else I knew, did all her own shopping, and made many friends in the town near to Highbury. Why then was she still in care? Simply, because there was nowhere else for her to go.

As with all the other residents I have written about so far, Eva was born too early in the century. Had she been born today, she might still have needed supervision to lead a full life, but she would not have been shut away from the rest of society for the rest of her life following the death of her mother. Including the time Eva spent in the residential establishment, she was in care for fifty-one years before she moved out to live in a home in the community. Unlike Lottie, Eva survived a few more years in her new home - Eva was a survivor! At 78 years old she could and did cope with whatever life threw at her.

These 3 old ladies were unknown to me … this photograph was given to me by Mary when I told her that I was going to try and write a book about her life and the lives of others in the same situation as herself. In the photo you can see the print overalls the ladies were required to wear at all times except on Sundays. You may also notice that none of the ladies have teeth! In the case of the early admissions, in some cases right up to when the N.H.S. took over Highbury, the removal of teeth was compulsory in the so-called cases of Mental Defectives. This was allegedly to prevent them from hurting themselves or others by using their teeth. Despite the harsh conditions under which these old ladies lived, I must confess that they look happy enough to be having their photograph taken.

HAZEL WARD

Of the three wards used for the elderly people who had lived at Highbury for many, many years, I have already mentioned the residents of two - namely Laurel and Brentwood. The third ward, Hazel, also housed females. In the days when it was frowned upon, the burden of pregnancy out of wedlock, causing the loss of jobs and subsequent destitution, and the possibility of being in moral danger rested firmly on their shoulders. Men did not carry the stigma of bearing illegitimate children, did not lose their jobs and become without visible means of support as a result of a pregnancy; and men were seldom considered to be in moral danger. In those dreadful days gone by, they sowed their wild oats without recrimination, and left the females to bear the confinement, the poverty, and the harsh sentence which in so many cases was imposed upon them. On Hazel Ward there remained women whose sad lives equalled those to be found on Laurel Ward - some even to surpass in terms of misery and heart-break. Take Dorothy for instance - she was born in 1912, and admitted in 1944, diagnosed as feebleminded.

Little is known of Dorothy's early life. She attended school until she was 14 years old, and could both read and write. Home conditions were unsatisfactory, and so in 1931 a spinster friend took Dorothy into her care. That same year they left their home town and moved to Brighton in order to set up a Nursing Home, where Dorothy was to be employed as a domestic help. In 1937 Dorothy returned to the town of her birth for a holiday, and on her arrival back in Brighton was found to be pregnant. No-one ever knew whose child it was, and Dorothy kept her secret for the rest of her life. She remained with her spinster friend until the birth of the child; also Dorothy's secret, for no-one ever told the sex of the child. A few weeks after the birth, the baby died, and Dorothy's behaviour was said to deteriorate. She wept constantly, and shouted and screamed — not an unnatural response for a woman following child-birth and the loss of her child within such a short time. The other factor in her deterioration was her inability to work — also, it would seem to me, quite understandable so soon after a traumatic experience. These factors led to a visit from members of the Brighton Mental Defective Department, and Dorothy was kept under supervision until she was returned to her home-town 1944. What form the supervision took was not recorded anywhere!

On her return Dorothy was admitted to Highbury by the Relieving Officer, dated 1945, so somewhere along the line a part of a year was lost. Following admission, there is another time lapse, for it is not until 1949 that we learn that Dorothy was reported by the Medical Superintendent of Highbury, as being in need of

Certification under the Mental Defective Act. The petition was signed, and in 1951 Dorothy was diagnosed as feeble-minded - six years after she had first been taken into care. Why, we must wonder, were there time lapses? Had Dorothy become a liability; was she capable of an 'outside' life, but was there nowhere for her to go? By now both of her parents were dead, her half-brother was a chronic bronchitic and also a stranger to Dorothy, and her other two half-siblings refused to accept her. Dorothy was described as timid and apprehensive; she did not know what £100 minus £13 equalled, nor how many pennies made a pound, but she did not deserve to spend the rest of her life locked away, which at the time of her diagnosis seemed inevitable. It was many years after Dorothy's admission that the hospital doors were unlocked, and the outcasts were allowed to creep back into circulation in the most degrading of fashions for anyone.

Dorothy remembers well the supervised walks into town, walking in twos, side by side in the formidable 'crocodile' line, with 'paid hands' to guard the pathetic stream of humanity. Had Dorothy been born today, she would have received medical help to overcome her condition following the birth and subsequent death of her baby. Her depression would have been recognised as common in women after confinement, and she would have been treated accordingly. She might have needed a short spell of care in a psychiatric hospital, but certainly not the thirty-seven years that had passed and those still to pass when I arrived at Highbury in 1974. Dorothy was obviously well trained in domestic chores - she continued to scrub and hand-wash her clothing long after modern equipment had made these tasks so much easier. She remained timid for all the time that I knew her, and kept herself to herself, but she blossomed with individual attention on the self-catering holidays, and it was then that we found the Dorothy who had been lying hidden inside her for so long. She had a good sense of humour, bordering on the cheeky, and was always smartly dressed, and her hair was always beautifully styled. In 1981 Dorothy was moved into a residential home, and lived out the rest of her life as part of the wider community, where she was totally accepted by her neighbours. I was told that she never overcame her obsession for performing her domestic chores the hard way.

How often have my children looked at me with open defiance, clenching and unclenching little fists wishing desperately that they could strike? How often have I felt the desire to slap my own mother when I have believed her to be unreasonable? Yet, my children and I are still good friends, and my mother and I overcame these episodes without permanent harm to either of us. Not so for Clara!

Born in 1904, Clara was committed to the County Mental Hospital by her mother on the grounds that she raised a brush to strike her. This was in 1924, when it was as easy to be rid of someone as it was to be rid of an unwanted garment. Before Clara was reported to the Committee of Care for the Mentally Handicapped, by the Medical Superintendent of the Mental Hospital, she was described as co-operative, harmless, and 'usefully employed' with cleaning and laundry. She could have been returned to her mother. Her mother did not want her, and so in June 1929, Clara was examined by an Inspector of the Board of Control and certified as an imbecile. There is no record of her ever attending school; she could not read and write, so why was he amazed that she could not name four large towns in England, did not know the name of the then Prime Minister, or how many half-crowns made one pound?

A J.P., under the Lunacy Act 1890, made a petition to the local Poor Law Institution, and Clara's mother signed the form for committal. Thus, in 1929, forty-five years before I knew her, Clara was admitted to Highbury. On her admission form was written: 'She is a Mental Defective who is detained in an Institution for Lunatics and is considered suitable for transfer to an Institution for Mental Defectives'.

Clara had become a neat little package to store away until some future date when someone would chance upon it. The future date for Clara was 1946, seventeen years after her admission! Her diagnosis was changed to 'feeble-minded', and she was again put tidily away. Seven years later, in 1951, Clara was considered for discharge. Her parents were both dead, and there was nowhere for Clara to go. She was to spend another thirty years at Highbury before she was offered a new home!

Clara was a sweet old lady, clean, respectful, helpful, and in possession of a very sharp wit. She had a 'boyfriend', Lol (Lawrence) on Brentwood Ward, money to spend, and was able to mix well in the local community. In 1982, aged 78, Clara and Lol were moved together into a Residential Home run by Mencap Homes Foundation. There were limitations as to how liberal we could be with ideas for our residents in the hospital, simply because it was a hospital, but care in a Mencap Home was as near to a 'normal' home as anywhere could be. Clara and Lol loved it! They found untold happiness with their new freedom, while still being technically ' in care'.

Florrie was born in 1914, the youngest child of ten. Her mother died when she was four years old, and Florrie was pampered by the elder children. She attended school, could read and write, but did not find work on leaving school and simply stayed at home with her father — her siblings were now married and had left the family home. Florrie's father re-married, and when he died in 1931, she only spent one more year with her step-mother. She was committed to the County Institution following a report saying that she was "wholly unable to work". Stepmother signed the form agreeing to Florrie's detention. This was in 1932, and the Public Assistance Board decided that Florrie was a suitable case for action under the Mental Defective Act 1913. In 1933 she was examined and certified as feeble-minded. The petition was authorised, and accommodation was found at a Farm Colony for Defectives in 1935. At this time it was stated that Florrie could read well, but, although she could write very well with her left hand, she could not write at all with her right one. Hardly a reason for being labelled feeble-minded, I would have thought, considering how many left-handed writers there are about today. Ironically, after Florrie's step-mother had signed away the life of her stepdaughter, she herself was found to be destitute and without visible means of support. She was taken to the same County Institution where Florrie had begun her term of care, and there she stayed until she died.

1n1944 when Florrie was transferred to Highbury she was medically examined, and asked to repeat three different twenty word sentences and lists of thirteen numbers backwards. She could not do either, and her diagnosis remained as feeble-minded. I should think that test would label a good many of us feebleminded today!

1952 is the next date in Florrie's records. This time she was asked 'Why is the Duke of Edinburgh not the king of England?' Nearly twenty years had she been locked away - should she have known the answer? Needless to say, she did not, and neither would a good percentage of the population of today, I should guess. In 1957, the living sisters and brothers of Florrie were approached regarding her discharge, but they all refused emphatically to accept her, and since there was no alternative home to try, Florrie stayed at Highbury. What a difference from the pampering of childhood.

Florrie was a well-built woman who kept herself very clean, and helped around the ward a great deal. She enjoyed sewing and was a good help with the ward mending - even in the 1970s clothing was repaired if possible, as the pocket money now received by the residents was not adequate enough to continually buy replacements. And so this was how Florrie spent most of her days, along with a little domestic work. She used to go into the local town with her ward friends, and attended the Salvation Army meeting once a week; she was quite a capable woman.

In 1981, Florrie, along with five other able residents, was moved into a half-way house to try out independent living. Despite supervision in the early days of this trial, it did not work. Perhaps she had been too long in an institution. Florrie and the others were then transferred to a residential home in the community, where there was supervision around the clock.

Gertie was born in 1903, and admitted to Highbury in 1949. Prior to this she had been an inmate in a certified institution in Derbyshire, and had been under guardianship in three different approved dwelling houses. On leaving school Gertie had quite a few posts in domestic service, but had lost each one because her father kept visiting her at whichever home she worked to 'interfere with her'. This eventually led to Gertie being diagnosed as an amoral imbecile in 1925, and she was removed from the family home having been found neglected. She was put under guardianship, and was used as a servant in all three of the approved dwelling houses. Why, I have to ask myself, was her father not removed, since his morals left a lot to be desired? As it was, Gertie alone paid for his lechery.

Father persisted in his lustful ways even whilst Gertie was living in the approved dwelling houses, and eventually it was decided that Gertie was no longer suitable for guardianship. Her diagnosis was changed to that of feeble-minded, and she was sent to her first institution in 1931. At her medical examination, Gertie knew that twenty-four half-crowns made £3, but could not divide 1 shilling and 3pence between ten boys.

On her transfer to Highbury, nineteen years later, Gertie began to spend two weeks' holiday every year with her sister - again largely due to a diligent social worker. This sister was asked to take Gertie to live with her permanently, but she refused to give total care; in 1958 she was approached a second time, but again she refused. The holidays continued, and were still taking place in the late 1970s...in fact, Gertie maintained close contact with all of her immediate relatives for all of the time that I knew her. In this respect, she was luckier than most of our residents, but I cannot help thinking that it is a sick society which allows the abuse of a youngster's body by her father and chooses to punish only the victim. Gertie was a happy person, content (as were so many of her peers) with her lot. She never did leave Highbury for a new home. Gertie died, aged 76, in her sleep and in her familiar bed on Hazel Ward.

Born in 1912, Gladys attended elementary school, and after leaving performed household duties at home instead of having paid work. In 1934 a health visitor called at her home, and was not satisfied with Gladys's life-style, and therefore began to pay the familiar quarterly visits. Gladys was medically examined in 1937, and diagnosed as feeble-minded. Her mother had died, and Gladys was living in lodgings with her father, who was a miner, just the two of them.

Her father could not offer suitable supervision, and still go to work, and so he applied for guardianship for Gladys in an approved home in Newark. His application was granted, but Gladys's G.P. suggested admission to the county institution - Highbury in the early days. Thus it was that in 1940 Gladys entered Highbury. Little else is recorded until 1952. During this year, Gladys's father was located after twelve years. He had re-married, and now lived with his new wife, a hospital worker, in a clean, good home. There was adequate control to consider discharge for Gladys, and the couple was willing to give it a try. However, the medical superintendent of the institution decided to delay the trial in case the arrival of Gladys in the home caused a domestic upset between the father and his new wife, who had not known Gladys prior to her institution days.

With this delay the chance was lost for Gladys, for although the couple was willing to accept her in 1952, they were no longer willing in 1957. They wished for her to remain in the institution (now a hospital) but gave her holidays in their home at regular intervals until they passed away. In one respect Gladys was lucky — she was blessed with a step-mother who did not shun her, but I have to wonder if she should not have been given her chance in 1952. When I left Highbury in 1988, Gladys was still a resident there after forty-eight years, and she finally died there a few years later. Why she was not considered for Community Care, I shall never know.

Now I shall relate the story of Ivy, for certainly hers was an eventful life. Born in 1921, she attended school and held several jobs in factories upon leaving, including one in the bottling department of a brewery for as long as four years. Ivy had four illegitimate children at the time of her first marriage in 1943. This marriage was doomed to fail — Ivy's new husband had married her bigamously, and by the time the police had told Ivy, he had already left her, and she was named as co-respondent in a divorce case.

In May 1945 Ivy married again — another failure! In November of the same year, her second husband was committed to a state institution, now a special hospital, for maliciously wounding her. Following this episode, Ivy returned to live with her father in one room — filthy, without beds, and having only old boxes for furniture.

In 1948 Ivy was admitted to a hospital in Mansfield for the birth of her fifth child. As a result of a report by the County Almoner, Ivy was transferred to a residential establishment close to the hospital. Here she was medically examined, certified as 'high grade' feeble-minded and recommended for admission to an Institution.

1948 was a busy year for Ivy. She had already served a term of imprisonment for child-neglect, and now she was before the court again facing the same charge. The case was adjourned pending a medical report. Later in the same year she reappeared in court, pleaded guilty, and was removed to the County Institution (Highbury) pending a petition under the Mental Defective Act 1913. The irony of it is that the petition was signed by her husband, still an inmate in the State Institution, and witnessed by the medical officer of that institution.

On her admission to the County Institution, Ivy was docile, willing to please, not grossly retarded, but guilty of a criminal offence. Her crime was that of neglecting one daughter, and causing unnecessary suffering and injury under Section 1 of the Children and Young Persons Act 1933.

Ivy's children were all removed to various homes, and we knew that two of the five were adopted with Ivy's consent. Of the other three, there is nothing recorded and Ivy herself did not know what became of them. In 1950 Ivy's father, now an O.A.P., was approached regarding her discharge, but he could not have taken on the responsibility at his age, and her husband was still an inmate of the state institution and could not therefore help. In 1952 an aunt offered to take Ivy into her home, but following investigation it was found that she merely required a servant, and so the medical superintendent declined the offer. Should Ivy have been given this chance? Would it not have been better to be a servant in the 'outside' world, than to spend the rest of her life in an institution, albeit the building was now called a hospital? A difficult question and one I would not attempt to answer. However, because of that decision taken in 1952, Ivy was still a resident of Highbury when I started to work there in 1974, twenty-two years later.

Ivy had a 'job' helping out in the staff dining room — a shrewd young woman (by comparison to most of our other residents who were much older) with an almost puritanical outlook on life. It was impossible when first meeting her to believe that she was the mother of five illegitimate children, so prim, proper, and prudish as she was. Ivy was an attractive woman, very sprightly, who mixed well with the local community. The nursing staff were shocked and saddened when she died from cancer in 1977, aged only 56.

As for Ivy's husband, he was transferred to a less severe institution in 1965, and made application for release to the Mental Health Review Tribunal. However he died in 1973, having spent twenty-five years locked away.

COMMITTEE FOR THE CARE OF THE MENTALLY HANDICAPPED

FOR THE COUNTY OF..

MENTAL DEFECTIVE ACT 1913.

CONSENT OF A PARENT OR GUARDIAN TO AN ORDER BEING MADE FOR PLACING A DEFECTIVE IN AN INSTITUTION.

....

I, ...of...

Being the ....of ....

A defective subject to be dealt with under the above Act, hereby consent to an order being made under the above act for placing h.. in an Institution.

Dated this...............day of...

Signed..

WITNESS...

....

....

....

....

This is a copy of the form which Ivy's husband signed in 1948 to commit her to spend the rest of her life in an institution. At the time Ivy was 27 years old and her husband was himself an inmate of the State Institution; was he therefore capable of signing away another person's life? Ivy was 56 when she died, with 29 years of life in care behind her and the possibility of a good many more had she not died so prematurely.

Despite the accounts you have just read, do not imagine that life in my time at Highbury was full of misery. Out of these tragedies emerged 'characters' such as will never be replaced. There was a 78 year-old who talked of charging 2 shillings and 6 pence (approx 12p) for a 'bit on the side of the embankment'; a 69 year old with an obsession for toilet rolls, and an 84 year old who rummaged in the garbage bins for scraps of unwanted food, despite being very well-fed. Each of them would recount tales of the past, funny tales, sad tales, re-living every beautiful or terrible moment over and over again.

Yet occasionally grim memories of the early days of poor-house life were very much in evidence. Can you imagine how it felt to be asked by an old lady (old enough to be your grandmother) if she may be 'excused', go out, come in, breathe almost? It gave a feeling of great humility to the listener, and out of that humility was born pity, compassion, call it what you like, the love of man for his fellow human beings: the love which had been missing for so long and had at last been found.

Standing at the back is Florrie, and seated below are Gertie, Doris and Ethel.

I could not mention Ethel in my book since so little was known about her, other than the fact that she and her sister, Lottie, seemed to have spent most of their lives 'in care'. No records were available to me, and all that I could learn about their presence at Highbury was 'they have been here forever!' The sisters were both in possession of great wit and humour: Lottie was very droll, whereas Ethel was infectiously funny, her humour, more often than not, directed at herself. Lottie died from cancer during my time at Highbury, and Ethel eventually moved into a community nursing home in the early 1980s. I can still hear her chanting her little ditty:

Ethel Hill, on the pill,
Never worked, and never will!

So many wonderful characters locked away and forgotten!

MOMENTS OF FUN

During the course of attempting to portray the lives of the residents of Highbury Hospital, I may have placed too much emphasis on the sadness to be found. There was great sadness, no one can dispute that fact, but over the years as staff attitudes changed, and major improvements were made to the buildings, it soon became evident that there was time for some fun too. It can only be hoped that a little sunshine filtered through into the lives of the folk to whom life had dealt a cruel blow.

As I said previously, do not imagine from my dismal descriptions of the lives of most of our residents that there was only sadness at Highbury. We had many, many moments of fun, both with our older folk, and the younger ones who replaced them when they died or moved on.

Mabel was 84 years old in 1976, a 'left-over' from the Poor Law, with very little recorded about her early life; she was as full of vitality as a two year old and never failed to amuse us. She lived to eat, and yet remained as slim and sprightly as a teenager. In the time it took to blink, she would have disappeared to the hospital kitchen to beg onions for tea. She never came back to the ward empty-handed, for if she wasn't given one thing she would take another.

Mabel, our 'borrower' of flowers and market stall produce and our eater of tomatoes sprayed with toxic chemicals. By the expression on her face in this picture, you can see the mischief in those beautiful old eyes – 84 years old and as sprightly and mischievous as an elf. Mabel was an outdoor person (more to 'borrow' there, I guess) and it was difficult to keep her inside if the weather was dry.

On one occasion Mabel was taken to the local market by a nursing assistant to spend her pocket money. On her return, her bag full of edible goodies, Mabel was reluctant to take off her coat. Why? Well, because up one sleeve she had two pears, two oranges, and the inevitable two onions, with the compliments of a market trader who blinked too often, and a nursing assistant whose eyes must have been closed all the time! Frequently in our field of nursing there was a shortage of staff, and Mabel was quick enough and shrewd enough to take advantage of this. When the pear trees in the hospital grounds were in fruit, she would take the window pole and march to the trees, lashing out at the forbidden fruit and causing the pears to fall. Of course if we spotted her in time, we stopped the march, otherwise we spent the next few days emptying her pants of undigested pears. Mabel 'borrowed' flowers too, not to eat, though with her even this would not have surprised us. In March every year, the hospital drive was a mass of golden daffodils, dotted here and there with fragrant wall-flowers, and being a great lover of all flowers, these were temptation itself to Mabel and she could not wait for them to bloom.

Laurel Ward was generally over-crowded with the borrowed blooms, though once again Mabel was fetched indoors if she was seen to be borrowing (not until she had already picked one or two, I must confess.) Mabel had worn a groove approaching the gardener's shed, because she had been so many times to beg for plants to decorate the ward — these were not easily borrowed as they were locked inside the greenhouse. She was seldom refused, but on one occasion while the gardener was finding a plant for her, she decided to explore his domain. She wandered into the greenhouse where he kept his prized tomatoes. Although Mabel could read very well, the words 'SPRAYED WITH TOXIC CHEMICALS' did not deter her. Before the gardener realised that she was missing, Mabel had completely stripped and eaten a whole plant! He rushed her back to the ward where the nurses began immediately to induce vomiting. Large amounts of salt were added to a mug of coffee, and Mabel said it was lovely and please could she have another drink. Thus it was necessary to don surgical gloves to encourage vomiting by tickling the back of her throat. By this time the doctor had arrived, and Mabel promptly reported the nursing staff for cruelty by making her sick!

The second of the two lovely photographs of Mabel shows her enjoying a walk in the snow on the field adjacent to the ward – well wrapped up and loving every minute of it.

Mabel was in domestic service prior to the birth of her illegitimate daughter, and remembered clearly the hard work involved in this life - getting up at 5a.m. to clean the grates and light the fires, and then non-stop graft until bed-time, sometimes as late as midnight. She often talked of her one day off every week - spent in her Sunday costume, always with hat and gloves, sitting by the Embankment. Mabel came from a poor family, but had a rich aunt near-by who remembered her poor relatives only at Christmas. This aunt would send food parcels - a 2lb. pork pie for Christmas breakfast, cigars for dad, sweets for the children, and a jugged hare for Christmas dinner. Holidays for Mabel were spent with her grandparents in the country and she could still name every flower and vegetable in their garden some seventy or more years later.

Tragedy struck for Mabel at 30 years of age with her pregnancy - the result, she claimed until her dying day, of the Master of the house where she was employed forcing himself upon her. The child of this sad union died six months after her birth - she was hydrocephalic, but Mabel had been at Highbury ever since the pregnancy had been determined, a total of fifty-four years when I first met her and with more to come. It was known that Mabel was capable of work, indeed she was quite an intelligent woman, so I cannot understand why she was not released to pick up her life again. Was it that she was still young enough to bear more children, and the way to avoid that was to keep her locked away? Who knows! Mabel was a fantastic old lady, loved by everyone and the recipient of more flowers and onions than anyone else I know or ever knew.

Despite her great age Mabel was moved into a community home in 1981. She lost her freedom to roam, she lost her friends in the hospital kitchens and gardens, she missed the blooming of the daffodils and wall-flowers, and needless to say, she didn't live for very long after her move from Highbury. Following 61 years 'in care', her spirit was finally broken.

How many toilet rolls do you suppose twenty-eight ladies could use in a week; thirty; forty; fifty? In one week we excelled! Seventy-eight toilet rolls came to Laurel ward, and seventy-eight were used! Mary-Jane was almost totally responsible. Relief staff hadn't a chance against her constant, crafty demands for "a doin's in the wotsit", loo paper, and yet there were never any to be found, nor evidence of there ever being any there.

Mary-Jane was diagnosed as feeble-minded with schizophrenia. That sentence sums up everything we knew about her apart from the knowledge we gained through knowing her. If there was occasion to reprimand Mary- Jane for pinching loo rolls, only after we ourselves had been reprimanded by the stores' manager, she would automatically become either Mary or Jane, and would blame the offence on whichever she had chosen not to be. She could hold a two-way conversation with herself adopting a different voice for both Mary and Jane, and it was quite amusing to listen when she was unaware of our presence. Mary- Jane was 'her own woman', she cared for no-one, she didn't go out of her way to please or impress, and yet everyone loved her. If only we could speak our minds as freely as she did and still be loved, what a stress-free world we should live in.

Although nothing is known about the early life of Mary-Jane, I do know that she ended her days in the care of Mencap Homes Foundation, residing in a lovely purpose-built unit not too far away from Highbury. I met her on many occasions after her transferral, and she did not change at all. What amusement she must have given to the staff of the home: she was a source of good fun, she could laugh at herself, and she brightened every day. I did often wonder, though, if the budget of the home could cope with her obsession for toilet rolls!

It was not only the residents who left lasting memories of my fourteen years of working at Highbury, but events too. One crisp November morning at 4a.m. in the late 1970s, the sister of Hazel Ward and I, accompanied by her mother and my husband, took four of our elderly residents on a twenty-four hour trip from Dover to Boulogne - unforgettable!

The trip had been organised by the local evening newspaper, and the coach was full of pre-Christmas shoppers. By the time we reached Dover, everyone on the coach knew everything about us - Harriet had made sure of that. The ferry crossing was quite rough, but how well they all coped - we must have been the only passengers aboard who enjoyed fish and chips while the ferry rocked and rolled. For weeks before, the main topic of conversation at the hospital had been the forthcoming trip to France, and for Harriet, Dorothy, Margaret and George it was the realisation of something they had never even dreamed of. They strolled around the hypermarket like seasoned travelers, wandered in and out of the boutiques, the boulangeries, the patisseries, and bought chocolates from a very exclusive store. Tired and happy, we made our way back over the channel and boarded the coach for our journey home. By now Harriet had got her 'second wind' and sang all the way back to the bus station. In the early hours of the morning, everyone else on the coach gave up on sleep and joined in with the singing.

Another first in the lives of the residents of Highbury was to go to the polling stations to vote in the 1983 General Election. What great fun the preparation for this event was! By this time a lot of the very old residents had moved on to other homes, and so it was a slightly younger group who made it to the polls. Valentine wanted to vote for his favourite male nurse — needless to say, he did not go to the polling booths! Stephen walked into the hall where the voting was taking place and cried "Up the Labourers", and after casting his vote pinched the pencils from all of the booths. It must sound very irresponsible of us, to the reader, but I can assure you that we only took four men to vote that day, and all of them were capable of making their own decisions with regard to which party they wished to have their vote. The hospital psychologist made a video of this great achievement, so somewhere there is a copy of this first step towards being accepted as 'normal' members of society.

To celebrate the Silver Jubilee of the Queen in 1977, I appealed over the local radio station for people with any musical talent to offer their services free of charge, to help us give a party on a scale such as had never before been seen at Highbury. The response was amazing! We held our party on the playing field adjacent to Laurel Ward, and it was opened by a marching band of at least thirty men, women, and youngsters. There were singers and guitarists and they all brought their families, and the field was full to capacity with revellers. For weeks before, the nursing staff had been raising funds (coffee mornings, market stalls etc.) to buy food and drinks, and we were able to feed everyone who so kindly gave up their time to be with us.

These are just a few examples of the fun side of working at Highbury - there were many, many more. Just a few years later, our resident population was going to change dramatically, although the younger mentally handicapped who came to us were going to bring challenges of a different nature. Fortunately they had been born in a time when help was available, when professional people of all disciplines were on hand to make their lives as near 'normal' as possible. The challenges were faced with hope and vigour - no longer just custodial care. The role of the nurse would change from over-protective guardianship to one of relaxed friendship and equality. This was a difficult adjustment for many of the remaining older residents to make, but when I left Highbury, the signs were good.

In 1974 my husband was referred to as my 'Master'; a couple of years later he was greeted by his Christian name, and welcomed to the ward like an old friend. My children were at home with all the residents, young and old, and their welfare was of prime concern. Birthdays were remembered, visits to our home were made, and the ladies of Laurel Ward became an extension of my own family. This was how it should be. What a long way we had come from the workhouse days, but what a long way there was still to go!

Only two of the ladies in this photograph were known to me. The two ladies I knew are Doris, seated to the left, and Maisie, seated in the centre.

Only two of the ladies in this photograph were known to me.....the reason for its inclusion is because you are able to see quite clearly the heavy, black, laced-up boots which were worn for working in the early days of workhouses. It is amazing that these boots, which bore the stigma of pauperism and homelessness, became the height of fashion in the 1980s....indeed my own daughter bought a pair, and I could never look at them without being reminded of the damaged feet of some of our old ladies who were made to wear them for hour upon hour of endless work.

The two ladies I knew are seated in the photo, Doris to the left, and Maisie in the centre. Doris's only 'crime', which led to years of incarceration in various institutions, was that she was a 'cripple' and unable to earn a living in the outside world. Maisie was an epileptic, and she too could not earn a living, and was shunted about from institution to institution for the whole of her life. How different their lives would have been if they had been born today, into a society where disability does not prevent normal living, and where epilepsy can be controlled by drugs.

Life dealt a bitter blow to women like Doris and Maisie and so did death! In the early years, even after the beginnings of the NHS, these women, and their male counter-parts, were given pauper's funerals and buried far away from the more fortunate who could provide for themselves, usually in some forgotten corner of a cemetery. Forgotten graves for forgotten people!

FINAL THOUGHTS

What can be said to end the stories of these forgotten people? Throughout the preceding pages, I have tried to compare their lives to the same situation in the society of today. That they would have fared better is without doubt. Most of their crimes (if indeed they are to be called crimes) are still prevalent at this time. Our society is called decadent and permissive by some, but let us not be guilty of committing our less fortunate fellow-men and women to wasted lives behind locked doors. We all realise that we must have prisons for true criminals, and special hospitals for those among us who are a danger to themselves or to others, but for those people who simply err in the human way, let us offer help and support. Sometimes we may object to the help which is given to the 'offenders' of today, but at least the help is there - unlike in the days when most of our residents were found guilty.

The doors of Highbury have been open now for many decades, but are the hearts of the public even though the times have changed? Even now, in 2002, can they begin to imagine or understand the utter emptiness we saw behind the eyes of our old people: the 68 year-old who knew that her relatives would visit on the Saturday before Christmas from 3.15p.m. until 3.30p.m., and not again throughout the year; the eighty year old whose sweetheart and the father of her illegitimate son (whereabouts unknown) died before the marriage, thus condemning her in the eyes of society; and the seventy-nine year-old who gave up writing to her relatives because the letters said the same things over and over again, and there was nothing else to say, and there was never a reply anyway. Our old ones were comparatively lucky. The local people had grown used to them over the years, and those who were able to get out and about were recognised in the streets and shops. Yet how many more were scattered about the rest of the country and did not know this recognition and respect? Even in more recent years the care of the younger folk who replaced our old ones seldom reaches the public eye, unless of course there are allegations of cruelty by the nursing staff, and so they too tend to be pushed into the background. A typical case of the ostrich burying its head - close your eyes and the problem isn't there anymore.

And what of Highbury? A building is only important in as much as it serves the people who use it. Highbury has served well for 187 years, providing in the beginning a refuge for the misfits and outcasts of a former society. Latterly Highbury has provided medical and surgical care, maternity care and care of the elderly, but until almost two decades ago, still sheltered beneath its roof, those who came when there was nowhere else to go. What a tale could be told if walls could speak! Now in 2002 medical, surgical and maternity care have been moved off site, and only care of the elderly, care of the mentally ill, and care for those with learning difficulties remains.

As with all old buildings, we had our share of 'ghost talk'. The 'lady in green' was said to have been seen often — by workmen demolishing the old lodge to make way for a new unit, and by orderlies and domestics involved in cleaning the finished building. Tall, erect, smartly dressed in a long green crinoline, she wandered in and out of the beautiful new rooms. Was she, I wonder, comparing the old to the new, the past to the present? Wandering around the cellars in half- light, with mice scuttling in the corridors and between the arch-ways, it was not hard to imagine a 'presence'. Would it be that of one of the tormented souls labouring long and hard in the kitchens below, with the stone sinks and tables which would have gleamed and shone in those days but now stood dirty and cobwebbed? Or would the 'presence', in her long green crinoline, be that of one of those who inflicted the torment on the less fortunate — 'cold charities of man to man' — aimlessly searching to end their own spiritual persecution? In death, the inmates would have found a merciful relief, but what of their guardians? I prefer to believe that if any were to suffer everlasting torment, it should be those who originally tormented.

No story of a hospital such as ours would be complete without a few words about the staff who worked in them. The care of these old people, and indeed of the younger ones, could never be called glamorous. All too often staff recruitment proved difficult. Glory is not heaped upon these nurses as it is in other fields of the profession. Daily battles are not fought against death, and 'cures' are not brought about. Instead the nurse is often obliged to witness humanity in its lowest form! Men, women, and children debased by their handicaps, revelling in their own excreta, noses running, mouths dribbling, and eyes rolling in expressionless faces. From this poor excuse for life, the nurse and her/his professional colleagues must try to salvage, strengthen, or modify a personality. They must help to assess the level of ability of the resident to learn and understand, and with the use of strict training programmes, the nurse's own skills and boundless patience must help the residents to achieve their limits. The task does not end here, for once the limit has been reached, it must be maintained. Success is very often elusive, and the nurse must be able to face failure after failure, tedium and frustration, without ever giving up on the thankless task.

As I said before, any publicity given to our field of nursing is usually adverse - never is a good job well done reported in the national press, and so the stigma attached to this branch of the profession remains. I know from personal experience that the majority of nurses are very caring and are doing a good job well.
In the first instance, our unfortunate residents were labelled 'mental defective' - idiots, imbeciles, feeble-minded. What cruel words! In an attempt to erase the stigma attached to the 'defectives', meaning faulty, the label was changed to 'mentally handicapped', but Shakespeare was obviously right in his suggestion that 'a rose by any other name would smell as sweet'. The label was changed again, this time to 'mentally subnormal'. 'Defective'; 'faulty'; 'subnormal'; 'below par'; 'handicapped' or 'at a disadvantage'. I always preferred the latter. Affection can be found in the word handicapped, and with affection, handicap can be overcome. In the late 1980s the description became

'people with learning difficulties', a more kindly expression to use, and one which appears to be more acceptable to public ears.

And so the nurses battle on, sometimes against insurmountable odds, often in the face of public criticism. They risk being bitten, scratched, pinched, and kicked in the course of their duty. They may listen to obscenities pouring from thoughtless lips, clean up the faeces, mop up the urine, get used to the stench of human excreta, and still they care. Through these nurses, the field of caring for those with learning difficulties will one day be held in high esteem, along with other branches of nursing, and whatever label is given to the residents, it will no longer be a word to whisper.

Hopefully Highbury will continue to serve, not to confine and punish, but to offer better opportunities to some of the most vulnerable members of our society.

JANUARY 2011

I had heard from friends still living in the Bulwell area that Highbury Hospital as I knew it had been demolished, and there was nothing left of the old workhouse. Plans to do this had been in the pipe-line for a few years, and so I decided to go and look for myself. My husband and I drove down the familiar hospital drive and saw a complex of new one-storey buildings where my old workplace had been. Needless to say there was more than a touch of sadness. Laurel, Hazel and Brentwood Wards were no more and there was no evidence to be seen that they were ever there at all. Gone too were the old buildings of the Poor Law Dispensary, and along with them the plaques naming those officials who had the power to bury alive in institutions those unfortunates who were unlucky enough to pass through the portals.

Yes, there was sadness, but there was also hope. Looking at the new buildings and seeing signs to assessment and treatment areas, it seemed that the days of human beings hidden from society for decade upon decade, was over. I am not familiar with exactly what is happening at Highbury Hospital in 2011, but to some-one, who knows the past so well, the future looks bright and Highbury is still serving the public almost two hundred years after it was built.

As we look forward to the future, let us recall the purpose of the earlier pages of this book to remember those who were not so lucky, to remember what a society can do to the poor and vulnerable among them, and to ensure that it never happens again. Let us be sure that sometime in the future no-one else need write an account of FORGOTTEN PEOPLE.